Empowering Organizations with Power Virtual Agents

A practical guide to building intelligent chatbots with Microsoft Power Platform

Nicolae Tarla

BIRMINGHAM—MUMBAI

Empowering Organizations with Power Virtual Agents

Publishing Product Manager: Pavan Ramchandani
Senior Editor: Sofi Rogers
Content Development Editor: Feza Shaikh
Technical Editor: Saurabh Kadave
Copy Editor: Safis Editing
Project Coordinator: Ajesh Devavaram
Proofreader: Safis Editing
Indexer: Manju Arasan
Production Designer: Aparna Bhagat

First published: July 2021

Production reference: 1070721

Published by Packt Publishing Ltd.
Livery Place
35 Livery Street
Birmingham
B3 2PB, UK.

ISBN 978-1-80107-474-2

www.packt.com

Contributors

About the author

Nicolae Tarla is an independent consultant focused on business transformation through automation, enterprise architecture, and digital transformation. He has architected and implemented business solutions for over 15 years for the private and public sectors, at both enterprise and SMB levels. With a passion for CRM, he has worked with multiple platforms throughout his career and continues to recommend the best business solutions for clients.

He was awarded the Microsoft MVP award for 4 consecutive years. He is actively involved in the leadership team for his local Dynamics 365 user group and participates in organizing local Dynamics 365 Saturday events. He continues to share his knowledge through his personal blog and other channels. His Twitter handle is @niktuk.

About the reviewer

Renato Romão de Souza is a Microsoft MVP who has been recognized as a valuable professional by Microsoft in the business applications category. He was recognized as Power Virtual Agents Community Founder and Power Virtual Agents Super User, for the contributions he makes in Microsoft forums on the Power Virtual Agents product. He is a senior Microsoft 365 developer focused on digital transformation with Microsoft 365, Power Platform, and other technologies.

He has trained over 2,700 students in Power Virtual Agents through his courses. He is also the community manager of the CaquiCoders, organizing technical events with speakers from the technical community. Also, he is an associate at **MTAC** (**Multi-Platform Technical Audience Contributor**) Brasil, bringing technical content to non-profit organizations, communities, and students in Brazil and around the world.

Table of Contents

3
Building Your First Power Virtual Agent Chatbot

Section 2: Leveraging Power Virtual Agents on Your Website

4
Creating a Power Virtual Agent for Your Website

5
Integrating a Power Virtual Agent into Your Website

6
Handling Authentication and Personalization

Section 3: Leveraging Power Virtual Agents in Teams

7
Building a Power Virtual Agents Application for Teams

8
Integrating the Power Virtual Agent into Teams

9
Serving Information from Various Sources

Section 4: Best Practices for Power Virtual Agents

10
Power Virtual Agents Governance

11
Power Virtual Agents Best Practices

12
Power Virtual Agents Administration

Other Books You May Enjoy

Index

Preface

Power Virtual Agents is a set of technologies released under the Power Platform umbrella by Microsoft. It allows non-developers to create solutions to automate customer interactions and provide services using a conversational interface, thus relieving the pressure on front-line staff providing this kind of support.

Empowering Organizations with Power Virtual Agents is a user guide to building chatbots without having to write code. The book takes a scenario-based approach to implementing bot services and automation to serve employees in the organization and external customers. You will learn about the features available in Power Virtual Agents to create automated bots that can be integrated into an organization's public site as well as specific web pages. Next, you will learn how to build bots to be integrated within the Teams environment for internal users. As you progress, you will explore complete examples for implementing automated agents (bots) that can be deployed on sites for interacting with external customers.

By the end of this Power Virtual Agents chatbot book, you will have implemented several scenarios to serve external client requests for information, created scenarios to help internal users retrieve relevant information, and processed them in an automated conversational manner.

Who this book is for

This book is for organization representatives looking to automate processes, relieve the first-contact workload of their front-line agents, and provide actionable results to employees and customers. Business professionals, citizen developers, and functional consultants will also find this book helpful. Some understanding of the Modern Workplace and the Dynamics 365 family of products will be useful. Beginner-level knowledge of what the Power Platform is and its main modules will also help you to grasp the concepts covered in the book more effectively.

What this book covers

Chapter 1, Introducing Power Virtual Agents, introduces you to Power Virtual Agents. It provides an overview of the technology's purpose, as well as comparing the specific Microsoft offering against other similar competitors' products.

Chapter 2, Licensing for Power Virtual Agents, discusses the various licensing options available for implementing this functionality.

Chapter 3, Building Your First Power Virtual Agent Chatbot, introduces you to the most basic Power Virtual Agent scenario. The most basic chatbot we will create will greet you and engage in a basic conversation, leveraging your responses.

Chapter 4, Creating a Power Virtual Agent for Your Website, leverages the basic knowledge we gathered in the previous chapter to extend the basic Power Virtual Agent we previously built to turn it into a fully functional agent. We will take a specific business scenario and create a more complex Power Virtual Agent. We will provide help to a user based on an existing knowledge library provided on a public site.

Chapter 5, Integrating a Power Virtual Agent into Your Website, discusses the various presentation formats and technical aspects of introducing a Power Virtual Agent into a public website. We will look at two different scenarios to present and trigger an automated agent on public pages.

Chapter 6, Handling Authentication and Personalization, delves deeper into the role of a Power Virtual Agent, with the ability to authenticate a user and provide personalized services. We will look at retrieving account details based on an already identified customer.

Chapter 7, Building a Power Virtual Agents Application for Teams, describes the process of building a Power Virtual Agent targeted at internal organizational stakeholders and team members. We will look at the differences between a public agent and an agent targeted at internal users.

Chapter 8, Integrating the Power Virtual Agent into Teams, presents details on integrating and leveraging a Power Virtual Agent from within Teams. We will build a Power Virtual Agent that will provide services through Microsoft Teams. We will show in this scenario how to integrate a Power Virtual Agent into Teams.

Chapter 9, Serving Information from Various Sources, discusses leveraging the available connectors to retrieve and present information in a conversation. We will look at a typical scenario for self-service when requesting information from your internal HR department.

Chapter 10, Power Virtual Agents Governance, looks at governance considerations when implementing the Power Virtual Agents functionality in an organization.

Chapter 11, Power Virtual Agents Best Practices, focuses on best practices when implementing Power Virtual Agents.

Chapter 12, Power Virtual Agents Administration, focuses on the administration of environments with Power Virtual Agents deployed.

To get the most out of this book

To take full advantage of the material covered in this book, you should have access to a Power Platform environment. You can achieve this by creating a 30-day trial or using an environment already created by your organization.

If creating a new trial environment, you should have some basic understanding of the Office 365 admin console, and the Power Platform admin console. Using these, you will manage users and environments as needed.

Software/hardware covered in the book	Operating system requirements
Power Platform tenant or trial – online	Since they are all Software as a Service, they are accessible via the browser and do not depend on a specific OS.
Power Virtual Agents environment – online	

Conventions used

There are a number of text conventions used throughout this book.

Bold: Indicates a new term, an important word, or words that you see onscreen. For instance, words in menus or dialog boxes appear in **bold**. Here is an example: "Click on **Continue** and wait for the system to complete all background processes."

> **Tips or important notes**
> Appear like this.

Get in touch

Feedback from our readers is always welcome.

General feedback: If you have questions about any aspect of this book, email us at customercare@packtpub.com and mention the book title in the subject of your message.

Errata: Although we have taken every care to ensure the accuracy of our content, mistakes do happen. If you have found a mistake in this book, we would be grateful if you would report this to us. Please visit www.packtpub.com/support/errata and fill in the form.

Piracy: If you come across any illegal copies of our works in any form on the internet, we would be grateful if you would provide us with the location address or website name. Please contact us at copyright@packt.com with a link to the material.

If you are interested in becoming an author: If there is a topic that you have expertise in and you are interested in either writing or contributing to a book, please visit authors.packtpub.com.

Share Your Thoughts

Once you've read *Empowering Organizations with Power Virtual Agents*, we'd love to hear your thoughts! Scan the QR code below to go straight to the Amazon review page for this book and share your feedback.

https://packt.link/r/1801074747

Your review is important to us and the tech community and will help us make sure we're delivering excellent quality content.

Section 1: An Introduction to Power Virtual Agents

In this section, you will start to get familiar with Power Virtual Agents, what the agents are, how they can provide value to an organization, and what the licensing requirements are, as well as building your first automated bot.

This section contains the following chapters:

- *Chapter 1, Introducing Power Virtual Agents*
- *Chapter 2, Licensing for Power Virtual Agents*
- *Chapter 3, Building Your First Power Virtual Agent Chatbot*

1
Introducing Power Virtual Agents

Welcome to a new adventure. You might have encountered various incarnations of chatbots over the years but not even realize what they are or how they work. This book is about to change all of that.

This is not a new topic or a fashionable episode in technology that will fade away. The time is now to start adopting these capabilities and putting your organization on the path to success.

In this chapter, we will focus on a historical overview of chatbots. We will be touching on the following:

- What is a chatbot?
- What is Power Virtual Agents?
- How does Power Virtual Agents add value?
- How does licensing work for chatbots?

Grab a coffee and let's get going.

What is a chatbot?

Chatbots, or simply bots for the context of this book, are not something new. They are almost as old as the internet. Of course, they evolved at different stages, taking various shapes and forms.

At a high level, the definition of a bot is *a piece of software, or an application, that performs an automated task or set of tasks.*

Way back in the beginning, chatbots were doing this by running a script or a set of scripts. This is nothing more than automating a set of commands.

If you think about it, it is pretty obvious how this would be valuable. It has been recognized that when dealing with repetitive tasks, leveraging a bot can not only take some of the workload from humans but also perform these tasks much faster and much more accurately.

This might sound familiar to those of us who have looked at how the personal computer was born. Not only have chatbots been around for almost as long as the personal computer, but they are now as important and prevalent as the personal computer, as we will see when we look at internet traffic consumption later in this chapter. As a matter of fact, the Encyclopedia Britannica defines a computer as a *device for processing, storing, and displaying information* (`https://www.britannica.com/technology/computer`).

But let's take a step back in time and look at some history. Bear with me here; this will set the necessary context for where we are going.

A condensed history of bots

The internet took shape in the 1970s. But it only caught the attention of the general public in the early 1990s. So, when I mentioned in the introduction that bots are almost as old as the internet, I was not lying.

Some of the first appearances of bots can be traced back to 1988. Yes, you read that right. Their preferred cradle at the time was a network called **Internet Relay Chat (IRC)**. For those of us with gray hair, or no hair left at all, this will be familiar. We used to spend entire nights exchanging information and finding things out, reading documentation and other materials shared, among other things. Various servers were powering different networks with multiple channels, some more friendly or interesting than others. Funnily enough, IRC is still around; you can always poke around and find out more about it.

Those early bots provided all sorts of automation in a channel. From keeping a channel active, recognizing users, and providing them with moderator or administrator status, to responding to specific commands and even returning automated messages or documents, they were ubiquitous in that space.

As a matter of fact, they were extremely important. Due to the nature of IRC, a bot was always used by an established channel in order to keep the channel open and to prevent malicious users from taking over that channel. At the time, these kinds of bots were run from machines with long uptimes, typically running some version of BSD or Linux.

As they started to show true value, they started to become more refined and to escape the confines of IRC. They also started to separate functionality. Some bots are designed for the repetitive execution of tasks, while others are more inclined toward conversation. And that's how chatbots were born.

Some of the first incarnations of bots outside of IRC though were in fact web crawlers. To be more specific, the first such bot was called WebCrawler, and it was created in 1994. It went from AOL to Excite. But the most famous web crawler was created in 1996. It was named BackRub and was later renamed Googlebot.

> **Important note**
> To find out more about BackRub, take a look at the following link: `https://en.wikipedia.org/wiki/History_of_Google#BackRub`.

But bots have not always been used for a good cause, as we will see in the next section.

Malicious use of chatbots

As bots became recognized for their power and usefulness, they started to catch the attention of various malicious groups. Just like everything on the internet, they started to take on a life of their own, varying based on the group that adopted them.

Besides the obvious valid and good use cases, bots started to be adopted and used for malicious use cases. Having the ability to perform a large set of actions in an automated way was appealing to all.

Between the years 1999 and 2000, several incarnations of malicious bots and botnets (groups of bots working in conjunction) started to appear, for which people were unprepared. Some of these activities started through IRC but then expanded into the wild.

The year 2007 brought us one of the largest botnets at the time, called Storm. It was estimated that the botnet infected 50 million computers. There were various programmed use cases and scenarios leveraged in the attack. While negative in its intended use, it did show that bots can really scale.

Some of these use cases include actions such as sending large numbers of spam emails, identity theft, unauthorized distribution of malware, DDoS attacks, bots for artificially increasing traffic and revenue on advertising, game cheating bots, and many more.

But it is not all bad, so let's shift gears and fast forward a little.

Fast forward to today

What we know and use today on the internet was shaped in great part by bots. Starting with the assistance provided on various IRC channels, or the web crawlers that put information at the fingertips of users, bots evolved into indispensable tools for many business use cases. The ability to automate processes, as well as the power to interact with bots through normal conversation, became an indispensable tool. As technology evolved, so did the capacity of bots. We can now create smarter, faster, and better bots. Bots assist us in doing our day-to-day activities, assist our customers, and provide a differentiator for businesses that adopt and use them wisely. The current business landscape has evolved to leverage bots at scale.

In fact, bots are currently adopted so much that some statistics show that out of today's web traffic, roughly half is bot-generated traffic. As technology evolves, exponential bot traffic growth is expected. This will be driven by technologies such as **Artificial Intelligence (AI)** and **Artificial Intelligence of Things (AIoT)** and the ability to implement conversational scenarios through natural language processing.

Let's just look at the Turing test, developed in the 1950s. It was meant to test the ability of a machine to have a conversation with a human in an indistinguishable manner from a normal conversation between two humans.

As AI-infused conversational chatbots have taken shape, their uses have extended into various scenarios, including the following:

- Messaging applications, either as part of websites or baked into various applications.
- Marketing platforms with a focus on external customers and potential customers.
- Company internal platforms focused on serving internal users and employees.
- Customer service scenarios targeted at helping existing customers.

- Healthcare scenarios for scheduling appointments, locating services, or providing basic medical information.
- Toys are getting smarter, with educational scenarios for various ages.

Chatbots are used in many other scenarios too.

In today's business world, chatbots will have an essential role to play. Let's look at the expected impact next.

Impact on organizations

As organizations of all sizes strive to evolve and compete with one another, part of their digital transformation strategy is to look at the use of bots.

Also known as enterprise chatbots, bots can serve various use cases in business, including the handling of customer-facing functions such as managing order status updates, cancellations and returns, account balance and payment processing, and customer service through automated support, all of which lessen the load on customer support and other teams.

Through integration with various automation processes, including **Robotic Process Automation (RPA)**, enterprise bots can not only increase customer satisfaction and provide better and faster services but also greatly reduce expenses, reduce workload on support staff, and serve various other purposes.

We do have to recognize, though, that while bots have gotten smarter and can do more, they are not in a position to replace humans. Hence, their position is ideal as a first line of contact, but processes will be escalated to a human team for more complex scenarios or scenarios that are not pre-determined.

Furthermore, the technological evolution over the last several years has brought us the democratization of bots and the bot creation experience. A multitude of platforms now allow non-developers to start creating basic bots for various scenarios.

To somewhat differentiate them from the old, negative connotation associated with the bot nomenclature, but also to more closely describe a specific category of services offered by bots nowadays, we find bots being referred to as virtual agents. Organizations have offerings of great value, such as the following:

- ServiceNow Virtual Agent: `https://www.servicenow.com/products/virtual-agent.html`
- IBM's Watson Assistant: `https://www.ibm.com/cloud/watson-assistant`
- Microsoft Power Virtual Agents: `https://powervirtualagents.microsoft.com/en-us/`

- Google Cloud Dialogflow: `https://cloud.google.com/dialogflow/`
- Amazon Lex: `https://aws.amazon.com/lex/`

And these are only some of the larger offerings. There is a whole range of solutions available from smaller vendors.

The differentiating factors between these offerings are their ease of use and creation, their ease of integration into various applications and services, their capability to leverage AI, their capability to resolve real use case scenarios in the most efficient manner possible, their capability to monitor their evolution and performance, and their ability to manage any associated risks. As AI is becoming more embedded in technology, ethics is a new topic on the table as well. The ethical consideration is at the forefront of a lot of new technologies, as we strive to make sure that the use of these platforms serves a real purpose and does not have a negative impact on people.

Some of the most common scenarios for enterprise virtual agents include the following:

- Support bots aimed at providing real-time help to customers
- Informational bots providing additional context in specific scenarios
- Application bots providing specific application access
- Enterprise productivity bots enabling organizations to streamline and integrate systems and processes

From a visual perspective, these chatbots are presented in various ways. It is often up to the design team to define the look and feel of chatbots on their specific target locations.

From a web presence perspective, the visual presentation often takes a cue from the overall web design, keeping with the tone of the branding of the respective site or pages where the chatbot is present. Let's have a quick look at some of the formats for presentation, as seen with a few of the larger providers of this service.

ServiceNow presents on their platform page a minimalistic chatbot at the bottom right of their page; it looks like this:

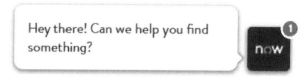

Figure 1.1 – ServiceNow chatbot

To make it obvious that a user browsing this page can engage with the chatbot, a starting message is also presented in a conversation bubble.

IBM, on the other hand, takes a more simplistic approach, presenting a simple icon:

Figure 1.2 – IBM chatbot

When clicked, a conversation window is presented to the user, as presented in the following screenshot:

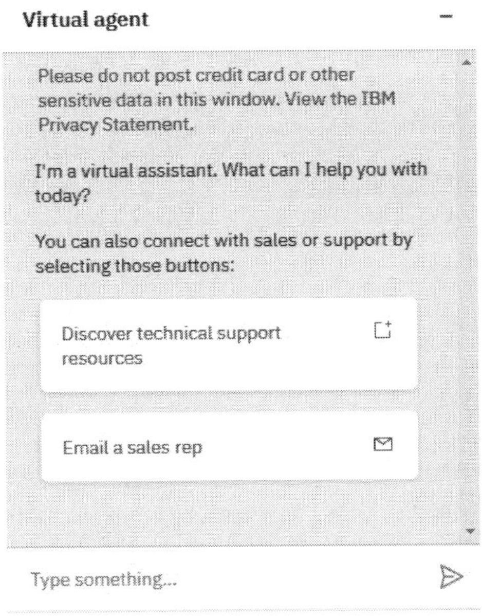

Virtual agent   –

Please do not post credit card or other sensitive data in this window. View the IBM Privacy Statement.

I'm a virtual assistant. What can I help you with today?

You can also connect with sales or support by selecting those buttons:

Discover technical support resources

Email a sales rep

Type something...

Figure 1.3 – IBM chatbot conversation window

Other organizations take a less conservative approach, by presenting the chatbot trigger with a graphic representing a robot, as we see in the following example from ShareGate:

Looking to migrate to Office 365 or a newer version of SharePoint and need a tool to help?

Figure 1.4 – ShareGate chatbot

Besides the custom-designed representations, there are many options for free graphics-depicting chatbots available on various sites that serve stock images. These can be used to put a face to your virtual agent.

It is not uncommon for these chatbots to receive a name and even a person's image or avatar in order to make them a little more personal. You might see messages such as the following, presented by the Amtrak virtual assistant:

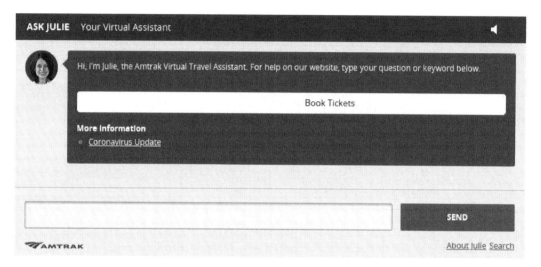

Figure 1.5 – Amtrak chatbot

Typically, you will see these chatbots presented at the bottom right of a web page. Note that not all elements positioned in that area of the presented web page are chatbots. Chatbots will not *always* be presented in that particular page area. It is simply a design decision rather than a standard. Historically, the bottom-right area of a web page was the space used by organizations for mailing list subscription buttons or social network links. A little bit of healthy competition for that screen real estate takes place sometimes.

Now that we understand more about chatbots and have seen how other organizations create and present chatbots, let's next focus our attention on the Microsoft offering.

What is Power Virtual Agents?

Power Virtual Agents is Microsoft's offering in the chatbot space. As organizations start to realize the importance of such a service, Microsoft joins the ranks of other vendors providing solutions in this space.

As we have just seen, there is quite the competition going on in the chatbot space, with offerings from all the big players in the industry, including Google, IBM, Amazon, ServiceNow, and others. Furthermore, there are offerings from small, specialized players with solutions tailored for various industries and various degrees of complexity or simplicity.

Around 2016, Microsoft recognized the potential of the bot offering for the masses and began its foray into this space with the introduction of Bot Framework. This was, at the time, a very developer-focused offering, with the ability to build complex bots using languages such as C# and Node.js as the core.

This robust framework was presented in conjunction with the Microsoft Cognitive Services offering, as well as the expansion of Cortana and chatbots into Skype. It is acknowledged that Cognitive Services played a role in the success of conversational chatbots.

The main components of Bot Framework included the following:

- **Bot Framework Service (BFS)**
- Bot Framework **SDK (Software Development Kit)**
- Bot Framework tools for development
- Bot deployment and channel configuration

As the resource needs for such a comprehensive offering are great, some Azure supporting services are leveraged, including the following:

- Azure Cognitive Services
- Azure Storage

The adoption of cloud services is now essential for such solutions.

Value to these offerings is provided through services such as the following:

- LUIS – natural language processing
- QnA Maker – answering questions in a natural way
- The Dispatch tool – allows for the selection of the correct tool for each scenario type
- Cards – complex presentational elements that include graphics, menus, and other artifacts to augment standard text presentation and provide a better user experience

The next evolutionary concept revolves around the ability of the bot to provide a REST endpoint to be called by the Bot Connector service. Having the ability to bypass the SDK, you can now create bots with other languages, such as Python. With version 4 of the SDK, support has extended to languages such as Python, Java, and JavaScript, along with the existing C# capabilities. All this was happening around 2018.

> **Important note**
> The Bot Framework SDK is in fact an open source SDK. This is a testament to Microsoft's renewed commitment to the community, and a stark contradiction to other organizations' walled gardens of proprietary solutions.

The most common channels supported by connectors include Facebook, Messenger, Slack, Teams, Telegram, Twilio, and many others.

Improvements and new features are continuously being added. For example, in 2020, a new implementation of Azure Blob Storage for better performance occurred, as well as better integration with Azure Queue Storage. Bots talking to other bots is possible through API communication or even through RPA.

Fast forward to the end of 2019, and Microsoft introduced the public preview of Power Virtual Agents for the first time. Wrapped in the Power Platform, it now provides users the ability to create chatbots in a no-code manner. Leveraging Azure AI and a specific toolset for building bots, the aim is to expand creation capabilities to allow citizen developers (your typical business users that do not have a development background), along with IT pros and pro-developers, to create and deploy chatbots with minimal effort and custom coding.

The new offering relies heavily on AI functionality to understand intention from existing conversations without the need to define all possible key phrases. It also relies on other features such as Power Automate to trigger specific actions on other platforms.

Another key aspect is the ability to generate and capture advanced analytics. You can easily track where the bot fails to provide the right answers and easily make adjustments to improve communication. A robust analytics dashboard provides deep insights into engagement over time, outcomes over time, resolution, escalation and abandon rates, as well as, when configured as such, customer satisfaction.

A lot of the analytics we were looking for in a regular customer service agent interaction are now bubbled up and presented to the administrator for the bot interactions. And this being a scripted process, you can easily go in and adjust the process as needed for better results.

The process to create new bots is now streamlined to the point where basic bots can be created by users with no development knowledge. Simple conversational bots can be created, monitored, and optimized by business users. This is part of a trend identifying these users as citizen developers. The bulk of the experience is built around a streamlined user interface that allows for configurable processes.

The developer role in the chatbot space

That is not to say that the role of IT pros or pro-developers becomes obsolete. Developers will always play an important role, especially when dealing with more complex or custom scenarios. The expectation is that developers will start to understand and leverage the tools available in their tool belts and use a no-code approach where possible. The advantages are obvious, with the ability to create processes and scenarios that require less effort to produce, less overhead in future maintenance, and a more streamlined product that protects the assets created from the unnecessary complexity that comes with custom development. This applies across the entire Power Platform and is not something specific to Power Virtual Agents. A configuration-first approach provides the ability to support the created assets in the future with fewer overheads and reduces the need to call upon a technical partner or internal pro-developer resource to support these assets in the future. It generally puts the power in the hands of IT pros, or even less technical and more business-focused people.

An important aspect is the understanding of the technology, best practices, and overall governance. While now we can allow non-developer users the ability to create business value through a no-code approach, we still need to enforce certain rules for better operation of the business assets created.

For those of us coming from the development world, this might sound a lot like the start of a typical Dynamics 365 (CRM) implementation, where a business analyst would start to mock up the requirements through simple configurations. As we've all seen so far, in some scenarios we could continue to build on top of those configurations, while in many other scenarios, we wind up leveraging those configurations only for the initial discussions with our customers and end up starting with a configuration from scratch. It all depends on the level of understanding of the platform capabilities from those resources that were involved in the initial stages of a project.

Overall, as those business analysts become more familiar with the platform, best practices, and overall design, more of what they produce in those initial stages will be reusable down the road.

From a user experience perspective, the bot creation and editing interface is simplified, as we can see in the following screenshot, which shows a brand-new bot I just created:

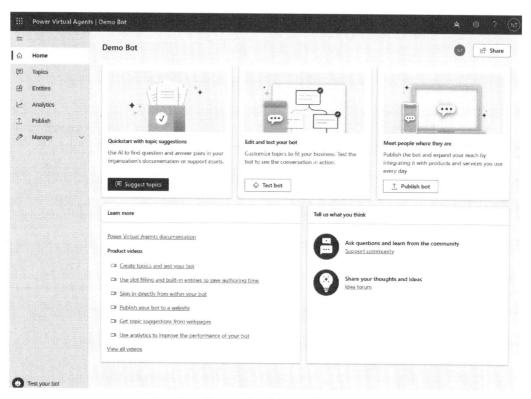

Figure 1.6 – Power Virtual Agents bot authoring

The left navigational area presents the various category options available, including the topics, the entities our bot will interact with, standard analytics on the performance of our newly created bot, and the ability to publish our bot to a selected channel. The **Manage** section provides detailed bot configuration options. We will be looking at each of those areas in more detail throughout this book, as we begin to build specific bots to serve various purposes.

The next area to the right of the navigation is the **Test bot** panel. This is where we can run and interact with our bot as we are building it, allowing us to validate the logic and the expected behavior. We can always show or hide this area as needed. Typically, we will keep this section closed to maximize the edit area while we are building our bot logic.

Finally, the right-most area covering the majority of the screen is the editing area. While on the **Home** area, this will present various details on how to get more information about building bots. This is a great place to start when learning about bot creation, as it provides links to the most relevant learning materials available from Microsoft.

As you move through to any of the other categories, you will find you are able to configure the details of the bot behavior. Again, don't worry if you are unfamiliar with these options at this time; we will inspect and analyze each of these options throughout this book.

Note that at the time of writing, there are two distinct scenarios envisioned for Power Virtual Agents. They are presented as the following versions:

- **Power Virtual Agents web app**: This is meant for creating bots that will integrate into existing or new web applications or mobile applications. This is what we saw in the previous screenshot and is aimed at users creating bots that will interact and engage with customers. These are, for the most part, publicly available bots. Of course, there is nothing stopping you from creating and presenting these bots on an intranet portal to internal users and taking advantage of internal authentication, as we will see in *Chapter 6, Handling Authentication and Personalization*.

- **Power Virtual Agents Microsoft Teams app**: This is meant for supporting existing employees of your organization. By definition, they are not exposed publicly and are only aimed at supporting your staff, team members, or any other internal resources. In many cases, you can leverage existing Microsoft 365 licensing, which includes the standard Office functionality along with several cloud services such as SharePoint, OneDrive for Business, Exchange, Teams, and others.

We will see throughout the book how to build bots for both these scenarios and will gain a better understanding of the differences.

Now we know what Power Virtual Agents is, let's look at its value and benefits.

How does Power Virtual Agents add value?

Power Virtual Agents is an integral part of the Power Platform, a robust offering from Microsoft targeting the no-code marketplace. As such, for organizations invested heavily in Microsoft technologies, it simply makes perfect business sense to obtain services that would keep them in the same technology realm. This provides easier maintenance, less of a need to reskill existing support and administration staff, and a better integration story across the board.

In addition, Power Virtual Agents leverages some of the same technologies that other platforms use, for example, Dataverse. **Dataverse** is the data model formerly known as **Common Data Service (CDS)** – it powers a few other solutions in the business applications space and can also be leveraged with other components of the Power Platform. This allows the creation of unified solutions, sharing data, and creating robust business processes unbound by standard application limitations.

Also, from a licensing perspective, the ability to leverage Power Virtual Agents with your Microsoft 365 license allows organizations to start taking advantage of these features without incurring any additional costs.

From a usability perspective, with Power Virtual Agents being an integral part of the Power Platform, you have the ability to leverage a large number of pre-built connectors and services to increase the capability of the services you provide through chatbots.

Finally, from a user experience perspective, the ability to use Power Virtual Agents through a common interface, similar to other Microsoft services, provides a level of familiarity to users. This greatly reduces the need for training and adjustments from one solution vendor offering to another.

These are only some of the highlights; there are a lot more benefits to implementing chatbot functionality using Power Virtual Agents, as we will continue to see throughout the following chapters.

In the next section, we will tackle the licensing aspect of Power Virtual Agents at a very high level.

How does licensing work for chatbots?

While this is not a comprehensive licensing guide, I want to start touching on this topic right from the first chapter. Licensing is extremely important to understand when designing solutions, in particular solutions spanning multiple technology stacks. Licensing Power Virtual Agents is tightly integrated with the Power Platform general licensing. We will be looking at more licensing details and how to estimate licensing requirements in *Chapter 2, Licensing for Power Virtual Agents*.

Microsoft provides a comprehensive Power Platform licensing guide that you should be reviewing to understand the intricacies and details related to licensing various components of the Power Platform. Power Virtual Agents being one of the Power Platform service offerings, it is also covered in this licensing guide.

Microsoft revises this guide with every release, and you should always refer to the latest version. At the time of writing, the current version is the November 2020 guide, which is available to download from the Power Virtual Agents pricing page at `https://powervirtualagents.microsoft.com/en-us/pricing/`.

Keeping in line with the separate offering for Power Virtual Agents, the licensing provides two distinct options for Power Virtual Agents for the web versus Power Virtual Agents for Teams.

We have a tenant license available for Power Virtual Agents, which covers the functionality for the respective tenant it is associated with. The user licenses are licenses assigned to bot authors. They are available at no additional cost on a tenant with a Power Virtual Agents license and can be assigned by an administrator through the admin portal. This is done through the Microsoft 365 admin center, as shown in the following screenshot:

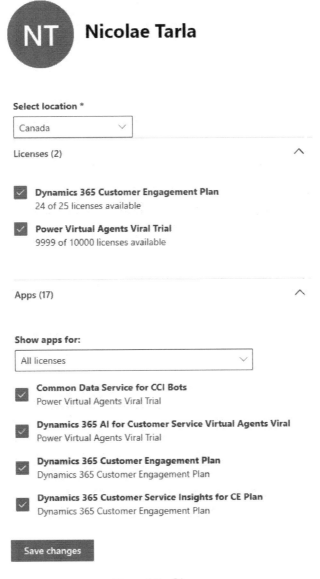

Figure 1.7 – Licenses

To view the available licenses in your tenant, you can navigate in the admin center to the **Billing** area and look at the **Licenses** tab, as shown in the following screenshot:

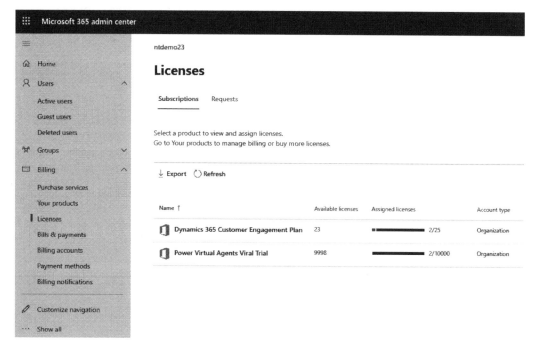

Figure 1.8 – Licenses tab

In addition to the standard Power Virtual Agents tenant license, an organization can purchase a capacity add-on if needed. This allows organizations to extend usage beyond the standard license limitations for sessions and storage.

Note that the default license allows up to 2,000 sessions per month and the following capacities for storage:

- Database capacity up to 10 GB
- File capacity up to 20 GB
- Log capacity up to 2 GB

These capacities are calculated on a monthly basis and remaining unused sessions do not carry over to the next monthly cycle. Storage capacity is fixed, though capacity add-ons can be purchased in increments of 1 GB as needed.

At this time, while organizations adopt and implement this functionality, some reasonable overages might be deemed acceptable, but organizations should plan accordingly for a possible future date when enforcement could be enabled automatically, resulting in potential business disruption. It is always a good idea to monitor usage and stay within the permitted licensing limits.

Since the Teams bot functionality is slightly different, the licensing is also separate. The Power Virtual Agents for Teams functionality is included with the standard Microsoft 365 licensing. Typically, the Enterprise and Business licenses will also include user rights for Power Virtual Agents for Teams.

With the Teams license, currently there is no restriction on the number of sessions or capacity. Capacity is actually calculated based on the Office 365 licensing capabilities. This might change as the platform evolves and Microsoft revises the licensing model.

Note that only some Microsoft 365 licenses allow chatbots to leverage Dataverse. In this scenario, once the capacity limits are reached, organizations will need to upgrade to a dedicated Power Virtual Agents plan to increase capacity.

In addition, another limitation of chatbots built for Teams is the ability to leverage only standard connectors. Premium and custom connectors are not available for these scenarios at this time.

Seeing how chatbots have evolved over time should now put this technology into perspective. We now have an understanding of how this technology was born, how it evolved to where it is today, and what the true business value is for current and future organizations.

Summary

Throughout this chapter, we looked at how the current chatbot offering was born, how it evolved through time to where it is now, as well as some of the good and bad uses of this technology. We continued our journey to the present day, looking at the importance of leveraging chatbots in the current business landscape and the value differentiator between Power Virtual Agents and Power Virtual Agents for Teams.

After we looked at the various providers of similar chatbot solutions, we narrowed our focus to Microsoft. Power Virtual Agents, being an integral part of the Power Platform offering, provides distinct advantages for various organizations and business scenarios. We looked at the different approaches to the creation of chatbots, based on the target audience. We now should have a clear picture of the difference between creating public chatbots aimed at customers and the larger audience and chatbots for internal organization users.

While we had a quick look at the licensing options and limitations, in the next chapter we will delve deeper into licensing concepts and look at some of the important aspects to consider when choosing your licensing model.

2
Licensing for Power Virtual Agents

Now that we have seen how chatbots were born, how they have evolved over the years, and how are they currently used by various organizations, let's delve deeper into how Microsoft Power Virtual Agents is licensed. We had a quick overview of licensing in the first chapter of this book, but here we will delve deeper into licensing and look at ways to estimate what the needs of an organization might be.

In this chapter, we will focus on two distinct scenarios, looking at both web use of Power Virtual Agents and using them in internal applications through Teams. The topics we will cover include the following:

- Introducing the licensing and pricing structure
- Understanding Power Virtual Agents and the Power Platform
- Understanding Power Virtual Agents in Microsoft 365
- Licensing considerations

We will conclude this chapter with an overview of how to approach estimating the needs of an organization that is just starting on this path, based on its current business processes and scenarios.

So, let's get going!

Introducing the licensing and pricing structure

Before we delve deeper into licensing considerations, let's first look at where all the licensing information is provided.

With every bi-annual major release of the platform's new features, a new licensing guide is provided by Microsoft. While licensing changes are not always major, you should review each new licensing guide and look at the nuances of each license presented every time.

It is not uncommon for the licensing guide to receive interim updates. In order to start with the most recent update, you should begin from the **Power Virtual Agents pricing** page, available at `https://powervirtualagents.microsoft.com/en-us/pricing/`.

At the time of writing, the **Power Virtual Agents pricing** page looks like the following screenshot:

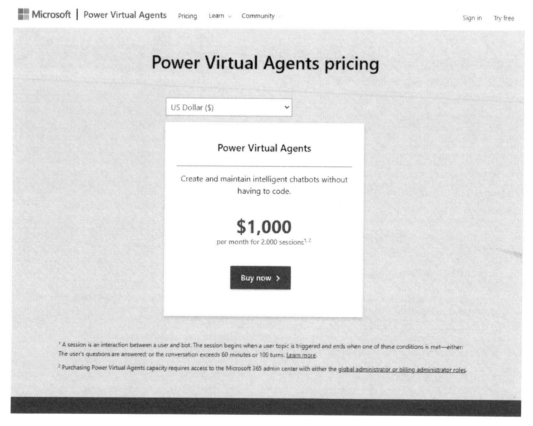

Figure 2.1 – Power Virtual Agents pricing

You can choose the respective currency for your country and see the respective price for the Power Virtual Agents plan.

Scrolling down, there is a quick description of the included features and limits of the Power Virtual Agents plan, as seen in the following table:

Explore the Power Virtual Agents plan

	Power Virtual Agents $1,000/month
What's included	
Create and maintain intelligent chatbots	1,000 bots
Sessions	2,000 per month[3]
Use <u>Microsoft Dataverse</u> (formerly Common Data Service)	10 GB database capacity[4]
	20 GB file capacity[4]
Enable your bot to take action	Power Automate use rights[5]

[3] Power Virtual Agents session capacity is pooled at the tenant level.

[4] Dataverse database and file capacity entitlements are pooled at the tenant level.

[5] Trigger Power Automate flows within the context of the chatbot. Includes access to Premium connectors.

Figure 2.2 – Power Virtual Agents plan features

Licensing is a very important subject to understand. When defining your organization's requirements, make sure you estimate the usage correctly. We will look at how to do that later in the chapter when we get to the *Estimating usage* section.

If you find that these limits are lower than your estimated usage, there is the option of purchasing the **Sessions** add-on package. This extends the usage limits and might be required depending on the expected exposure.

Finally, for additional details, Microsoft provides a downloadable licensing guide PDF, which you can take with you and study offline, or additional details in the Docs portal. The Docs portal is where all documentation is available, including not only how to approach licensing, but also how to build Power Virtual Agents in the most efficient manner. You will find technical documentation there, as well as **Citizen Developer** materials.

And speaking of learning materials, the Learn portal provides good, step-by-step materials in the form of learning paths and modules that are invaluable. It can be accessed at `https://docs.microsoft.com/en-us/learn/browse/?expanded=power-platform&products=power-virtual-agents`.

Let's next see the moving parts and considerations we need to be aware of when creating Power Virtual Agents chatbots.

Understanding Power Virtual Agents and the Power Platform

As mentioned previously, at the time of writing, Power Virtual Agents is the newest member of the Power Platform family of products. Our first scenario looks at the functionality available with the Power Platform. As such, licensing aligns with the general Power Platform model, as you can see in the specific guide. The guide covers all modules of the Power Platform, and you should focus your attention on the Power Virtual Agents section for this topic.

As a new member of the Power Platform family, you will notice that the licensing of Power Virtual Agents is slightly decoupled from the other Power Platform services. As of December 31, 2020, Microsoft has revamped the generic Power Platform licensing, dropping certain older plans in favor of newer packaged services. This is part of an ongoing process where Microsoft is taking feedback from the community at large, along with usage statistics and other influential factors. The new Power Platform licensing model moves towards a per-user and per-app plan. Still, Power Virtual Agents is licensed differently. We will see in a moment some of the reasons why.

If your organization does not offer Power Platform capabilities but you still want to experiment with these features, the next section looks at some ways to obtain temporary access for learning purposes.

Getting access to Power Platform

For those that want to simply try the features or learn by practicing, you have the ability to create a free 30-day trial. This can also be extended if needed.

In addition, Microsoft offers a free Community Plan. This is aimed at developers, IT staff, and citizen developers. It provides you with access to learn and upskill on Power Apps, Power Automate, and Microsoft Dataverse. More information is available at `https://powerapps.microsoft.com/en-us/communityplan/`.

Note that a Power Virtual Agents license is only required for users that will actively participate in creating and editing chatbots.

Let's revisit licensing considerations next.

Power Platform licensing expanded

There is a distinction to be made here between the user license and the actual Power Virtual Agents license. These work in conjunction but are managed differently.

First off, in order to be able to leverage the functionality of Power Virtual Agents, you will need to purchase a Power Virtual Agents application license. This license is a tenant license, meaning that once purchased and applied to your tenant, it allows you to create and run the Power Virtual Agents functionality.

If you expect higher volumes than what the standard license offers, you should also purchase a **Capacity add-on**. We will look at how to estimate your needs in the *Licensing considerations* section of this chapter.

In addition, when purchasing the tenant license, you should also request the Power Virtual Agents user licenses. They are available at no additional cost but are required to assign editors.

It is strongly recommended to purchase the tenant license and the capacity add-on together as it makes for a much smoother onboarding process.

Let's see next how imposed limits affect licensing and platform features' availability.

Imposed limits on Power Platform

One of the most common limitations you might soon hit when using Power Virtual Agents is the **Sessions limit**. The default plan includes up to 2,000 sessions per tenant per month. As the location where you choose to place your bot encounters increases traffic, the likelihood of your agent being used more frequently increases. This is especially relevant in customer support scenarios.

But what is a session you might ask? A **session** is defined as one end-to-end interaction between a user and your agent. This is counted from the moment one topic is triggered. This is basically the first interaction where the agent is activated. The end of a session is when a user's questions have been successfully answered and the conversation ends, which is an ideal situation.

In order to limit exposure and avoid uncommon scenarios, several other limits on a session have been added. For example, one limit is that a session can be considered complete when it exceeds 60 minutes in length or 100 **turns** (an exchange between a user and the bot).

Another limit included is that a session ends if it starts but does not complete with a successful outcome. In such a situation, the session falls under the previously described rule, and it is timed out after the specified amount of time.

It is important to understand that, while capacities are enforced monthly, any unused license allocation is NOT carried over from one month to the next.

In the November 2020 licensing guide, Microsoft tackles the overages subject by stating that technical enforcement of limits will be in place for usage that is significantly over the purchased capacity. This could include possible service stoppages if needed. The good news is that, reading between the lines, a certain level of reasonable coverages will be accepted. This is an important aspect, as this is a service open to the public, and especially at the beginning of the service, it might be handy to estimate expected volumes of usage.

Let's have a look at assigning licenses to users next.

Managing Power Platform licensing

Licensing management for Power Virtual Agents is handled in a similar way to other licensing management activities for the Power Platform and other services. This is done from the Microsoft 365 admin center.

You can navigate to `https://portal.office.com/` and find the Admin link on the navigation bar, as shown in the following screenshot:

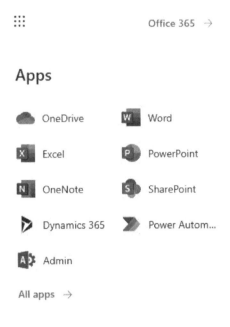

Figure 2.3 – Office 365 navigation

Once in the Microsoft 365 admin center, navigate to the **Users** area, expand it, and select one of the available options, depending on who you want to assign licenses to. The options are as follows:

- **Active Users**
- **Guest Users**
- **Deleted Users**

You will typically want to assign a license to an active user within your organization, so choose **Active Users**.

A listing of all users is presented, and you will want to select a specific user to assign a new Power Virtual Agents license. Once you select a user, a screen overlay is presented on the right side. Navigate to the **Licenses and apps** tab on it, as presented in the following screenshot:

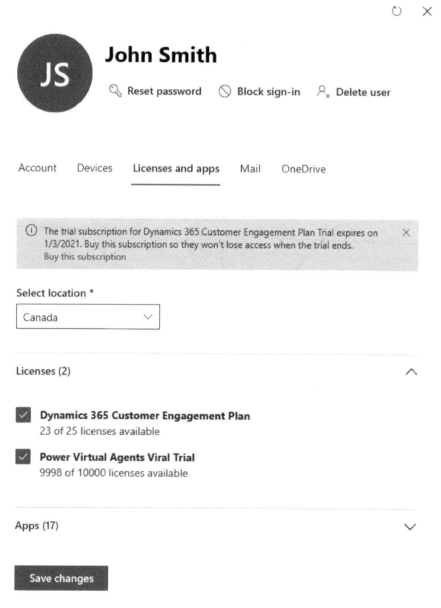

Figure 2.4 – User licensing management

Change the location if needed and select from the expanded **Licenses** area the Power Virtual Agents license checkbox. This will assign a license to the respective user, as desired.

You can also see here the total number of available licenses.

Part of organizational license management standards should be setting up processes for releasing licenses from users once they are not needed, as well as defining a threshold past which you should consider purchasing new licenses.

Let's next see the difference when dealing with the Power Virtual Agents functionality available with Microsoft 365.

Understanding Power Virtual Agents in Microsoft 365

For the second scenario, where we leverage Power Virtual Agents for Teams, the licensing is different than the standard Power Platform. User rights are included with your standard Office 365 licenses. Of note is that not all Office 365 licenses include the ability to leverage Power Virtual Agents for Teams.

Office 365 licenses that include access to Dataverse for Teams will typically also include user rights for Power Virtual Agents for Teams. These include the following:

- Standard **Enterprise** (**E**) licenses, such as the E1, E3, and E5.
- Business licenses such as the Business Basic, Business Standard, and Business Premium licenses.
- Some of the education licenses include user rights for Power Virtual Agents, including the A3 and A5 licenses for Faculty and Students.

When using Power Virtual Agents for Teams, you can create and deploy chatbots in Teams only. You have no session limits with a standard subscription, as opposed to only 10 per user for every 24 hours in a tenant for Teams.

An important aspect of leveraging Power Virtual Agents, both in Teams and for public consumption, is the ability to leverage Power Automate. That being said, there are some distinct differences between the two use cases. When deploying Power Virtual Agents for Teams, due to the nature of the scope, there is no access to an on-premises data gateway. That will become obvious once you understand that deploying within Teams has a target audience of internal users only, and there is no need for the gateway configuration.

Furthermore, Power Virtual Agents for Teams only has access to **Standard** connectors. These connectors are classified in **Standard**, as well as **Premium** and **Custom** connectors. With a Teams license model, you only have access to **Standard** connectors, which allow you, for the most part, integration with other Office 365 services.

From a capacity perspective, the default capacity limitations are per tenant, and include the following limitations:

- Dataverse database capacity limited at 10 GB

- Dataverse file capacity limited at 20 GB

- Dataverse log capacity limited at 2 GB

These limits are there not only from a billing perspective but also as an incentive to create more efficient processes that are built in a non-wasteful manner. You should try to understand concepts related to governance and the efficient creation of Power Virtual Agents before embarking on the path to create chatbots.

You might ask what each of those three limitations means. Let's have a quick look at each category.

Dataverse database capacity

The database capacity represents the ability to store definitions for your data model, as well as actual data. If we look at the creation of a chatbot in Power Virtual Agents, one of the tabs on the navigation is called **Entities**, as seen in the following screenshot:

Figure 2.5 – Power Virtual Agents Entities tab

Your default chatbot configuration will come with a set of prebuilt entities, but you can add your own as needed. We will look at that set of functionalities as we progress through the book.

Dataverse file capacity

The file capacity represents the storage of attachments to notes or emails, as available with the Power Platform and other Dynamics family products. These attachments typically include files such as documents, images, videos, PDFs, or other files.

A way to make your design more efficient is to leverage an external storage mechanism rather than using the default attachment to notes, but we will touch on that in *Chapter 4, Creating a Power Virtual Agent for Your Website*, when we look at building a more complex chatbot.

Dataverse log capacity

Finally, the log capacity refers to storing details on system data changes in the system. This could be either part of auditing or for reporting capabilities. This is an important aspect of organization governance and compliance, so it should be taken into consideration from the beginning of the process when planning governance and estimated costs.

Let's review some licensing considerations when planning for new Power Virtual Agents chatbots next.

Licensing considerations

In this section, we'll look at a simplified example of estimating usage for a new Power Virtual Agents chatbot. We will take into consideration expected capacity usage and come up with an estimate that will guide us in deciding our expected overall cost and usage.

The scenario

In this scenario, we will look at an organization that is just getting started with Power Virtual Agents, and how to find a more efficient way to estimate possible usage. We will focus our attention on the service department of our hypothetical organization. Our team is swamped with support requests from existing product users. Instead of increasing the team size, we looked at various ways to optimize and simplify our agents' work.

One initiative that was already implemented is the creation of a **Knowledge Base** section on our public website. We have spent a lot of effort in creating documentation to walk customers through installation and debugging procedures to fix issues. We have obviously observed a slight reduction in the time spent by our agents engaging with customers, as instead of staying on the phone and walking the client through all the steps, we can now just point them to a document that does just that.

Still, the amount of inbound support requests remains similar. We generate new support tickets from those, and an agent has to handle each one of those. For the most part, it is simply a matter of pointing the customers to the respective **Knowledge Base** article. This involves our agent opening the autogenerated support incident record, looking at the details, searching for the associated Knowledge Base article or simply retrieving it based on the automated suggestions provided by the system, and responding via email with a link to the article. The other scenario is inbound calls for support, where our agent picks up the call, creates the support incident, and follows the same path.

But how can we simplify that process, and reduce the load on our agents even more?

Offloading the first contact to a Power Virtual Agent chatbot is a great way of doing just that. We can now provide a new chatbot on the public support site. Customers looking for help can engage with this chatbot, describe their problem, and automatically receive a reference link to the related Knowledge Base article. This can dramatically reduce the load on our agents, while providing faster and more efficient support to our customers. Sounds like a win-win situation.

Let's have a look at one way to determine the licensing impact based on this approach.

Estimating usage

Estimating usage is an aspect of design that you will become more familiar with as you start implementing more real-life scenarios. For now, we are looking at a simplified theoretical scenario for guidance.

This will be a mathematical calculation, making some assumptions while taking into consideration actual numbers. Before embarking on this, make sure you have the correct numbers from your support team, as needed.

We start by first defining our analysis period. The larger the range, the more accurate your results will be. You must strike a balance though between accuracy and the effort needed to analyze a large batch of data.

In our scenario, we want to analyze the data over the last calendar year. This will give us a good idea of the seasonal spikes as well as capturing a large enough range of data.

Let's assume that we have a total of 50,000 support requests per year.

Of course, you should also take into consideration the annual growth year over year. Analysis shows that we have an increase of 10% year over year.

Further analysis of the support requests over the last calendar year shows that 20% of our cases were handled on the first touch, by forwarding documentation or providing links to our existing Knowledge Base articles.

These are the candidates for our newly created Power Virtual Agents chatbot. This means that we are looking at:

50,000 x 0.20 = 10,000 sessions

Out of these 10,000 possible support requests, and based on the demographics of our customers, we find that 30% are tech-savvy customers that could potentially take advantage of our chatbot functionality. You can determine this through demographics analysis, as well as by sending to a subset of your customers a survey.

Consequently, we now have:

10,000 x 0.30 = 3,000 potential sessions on your chatbot

Take into consideration, let's say, a 50% margin for adoption over the first year. This will reduce the numbers as follows:

3,000 x 0.50 = 1,500 runs

Add to that the 10% year-over-year increase in support requests and you will have:

1,500 x 1.10 = 1,650 sessions

Finally, get your numbers by month by dividing the number by 12 months.

This result puts you in the brackets of the standard Power Virtual Agents licensing model, with no need to add a **Capacity add-on**.

Of course, we have grossly simplified this calculation and have intentionally omitted other aspects that could be considered. This scenario is for simplicity.

This approach allows us to determine our initial capacity needs. Once we launch our chatbot, we can then keep monitoring the usage by going to the **Analytics** section on our Power Virtual Agents portal, and looking at the **Billing** tab, as seen in the following screenshot:

Figure 2.6 – Power Virtual Agents Analytics

The preceding screenshot shows the analytics on a freshly created chatbot, but we will see later in the book, when we build bots, how data starts to light up this section.

This should give you a high-level idea of how to tackle estimation. This is not the de facto template for calculations, and various business considerations will have an impact on how you approach calculating your estimates.

Summary

Throughout this chapter, we looked at the various licensing options and considerations when implementing Power Virtual Agents. We started our foray by looking at the licensing acquisition and defined tiers of usage for Power Virtual Agents. We looked at the default tenant license, as well as the ability to purchase a **Capacity add-on** when needed.

Next, we looked at the Power Virtual Agents for Teams licensing model and some of the important differences from regular public Power Virtual Agents.

We then looked at one scenario to estimate your potential usage when starting fresh with Power Virtual Agents.

When maintaining existing Power Virtual Agents chatbots, we have tools included with the platform to allow us to monitor usage and licensing compliance. We will analyze those in more detail as we start building chatbots in the following chapters.

In the next chapter, we will present the creation of your first Power Virtual Agents chatbot.

3
Building Your First Power Virtual Agent Chatbot

With a general understanding of how to license **Power Virtual Agents** (**PVA**), as we saw in the previous chapter, we are finally ready to get to the meat of the PVA build and see how we can build our first PVA.

But before we delve right into it, we will first look at how to set up a sandbox environment for us to work in; this will be our playground for the rest of this book.

This chapter will focus on the following topics:

- Completing the initial setup
- Knowing your environment
- Creating a Power Virtual Agent
- Publishing a Power Virtual Agent

At the end of this chapter, we will have built our first PVA. While this will be the most simplistic scenario, this is the base we will be building upon in the following chapters.

So, let's get going!

> **Important note**
>
> Note that your typical trial environment is available for 30 days, so if you extend beyond that, you can either create a new trial or request an extension to your trial from Microsoft support.

Completing the initial setup

Just like everything in life, let's start at the beginning. Before we create our first PVA, we need to obtain an environment and perform a little bit of setup.

If you already have an organization account, also called a work or school account, you can have an admin assign you a license to provide you access to PVA. If you do not, follow the next steps to create a trial tenant with such an account.

Creating a trial tenant for an organization account

If you only have a personal email address, you cannot directly sign up for a trial, as it requires an organization account. You must take a few extra steps to create an organization account first. The easiest way is to create a Dynamics trial, which will give you an organization account in an Azure Active Directory tenant, and then create your PVA trial based on that.

To create a Dynamics trial, follow these steps:

1.   Navigate to `https://trials.dynamics.com/`.

2.   Select the **Sign up here** link, as shown in the following screenshot:

Are you signing up on behalf of a customer or using this trial for development purposes? Sign up here.

Work email * ⓘ

Phone number *

GET STARTED >

Figure 3.1 – Sign-up screen

3. In the next prompt, continue by selecting the option labeled **No, continue signing up**:

Figure 3.2 – Continue signing up

4. You will be guided through a wizard to create a new tenant, along with a business account, as seen in the following screenshot:

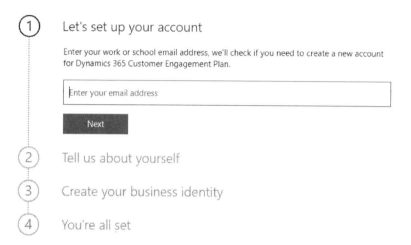

Figure 3.3 – Tenant creation wizard

The wizard is self-explanatory, but it is worth noting that in *Step 3* of this wizard, you will create the business account that you can use going forward to enable your PVA instance.

At this stage, you have an organization account and are ready to create your PVA trial.

Creating a PVA trial

Once you have your organization account, you are ready to create your PVA trial. To sign up, follow these steps:

1. Navigate to the following URL: `https://aka.ms/TryPVA`.

2. You are presented with the default landing page, where you will find the **Try free** link in the top right, as seen here:

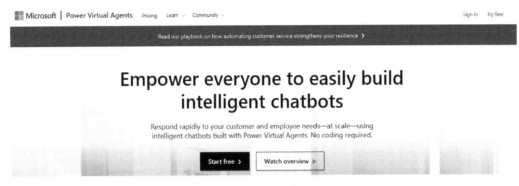

Figure 3.4 – PVA landing page

3. Simply follow the simple wizard prompts and shortly you will have your PVA environment ready to use.

> **Important note**
>
> In a tenant, the administrator could choose to disable self-service sign-up for PVA. This is typically an organization-wide policy, and you will need to adopt a different approach. Reach out to your administrator or create a new organization account as described in the *Creating a trial tenant for an organization account* section.

4. The last step in spinning up your PVA environment is the creation of your first agent. Give it a simple name to identify it as your first agent. I have named mine **MyFirstBot**, as you can see in the following screenshot, but you can choose any name that makes sense for you. You cannot change the language once it's set up, so make sure to select this correctly from the beginning:

> **Important note**
>
> An agent created in one environment can be moved to another by exporting and importing it into the new environment. Create your bot in a development environment before moving it to its final destination.

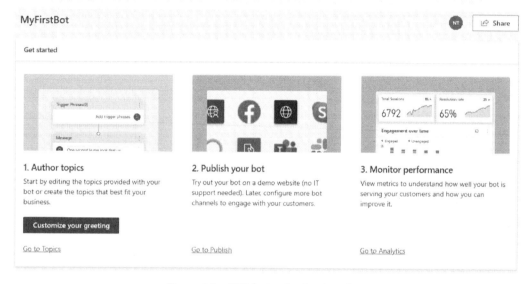

Figure 3.5 – PVA bot authoring interface

Now you have your first agent and are presented with the main editing canvas. Let's review a few areas of this editor in the next section.

Knowing your environment

Looking at the editor window can be a little daunting at first. Let's see what each component is and how to navigate around:

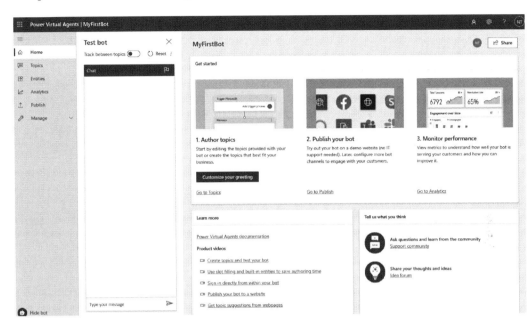

Figure 3.6 – PVA editor window

Starting at the very top, we have the banner with the standard Microsoft 365 waffle menu, followed by the PVA product name and your new agent name.

Further to the right, you find the little bot icon, which opens up the **Bots** menu:

Figure 3.7 – Bots menu

Here you can see the environment you are building in, the current agents already in the selected environment, as well as the option to create a new agent, as seen in the following screenshot:

Figure 3.8 – Bots in the environment

> **Important note**
> Note that the user interface uses the term *Bot* to represent a virtual agent. The terms can be used interchangeably, with the name *Agent* being a more recent synonym for *Bot*.

Further to the right of *Figure 3.7*, we find the cog settings icon, which expands a **Settings** menu:

Figure 3.9 – Bot settings area

Finally, further to the right of *Figure 3.7*, you have the **Help** menu and your user profile card, which is the same as within any Microsoft 365 tenant interface.

Further down and to the left of the editor window, you will find the main navigation menu, as shown in the following screenshot:

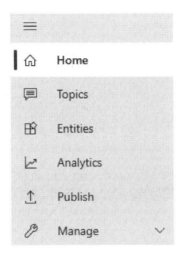

Figure 3.10 – Bot editing navigation

Let's see at a high level what each option is:

- **Home** is where we see the generic bot details.

- **Topics** is where we can review the existing topics created, as well as creating new topics and enabling or disabling some of the custom-created topics. A topic is a definition of how a bot interacts with a user in a conversation.

- **Entities** is where we see how we leverage data storage tables.

- **Analytics** presents the details on the usage in a manner that allows us to make decisions about performance, best use cases, and changes we might want to consider making to the bot.

- **Publish** allows us to publish a custom bot to make it available to users.

Further down, at the bottom of the navigation area, you will find the **Hide Bot/Test your bot** button, as seen here:

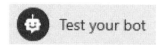

Figure 3.11 – Bot testing button

You will use this a lot while building agents, as it opens a view into how this agent will behave in real life. This option is a simple toggle that shows or hides the testing area, as shown in the following screenshot:

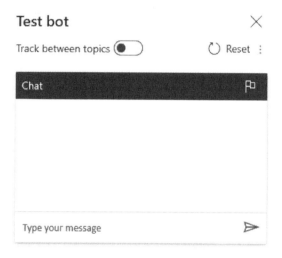

Figure 3.12 – Bot testing area

Using this area, you will determine whether the bot behaves as expected, whether the responses are in accordance with the design, or whether any adjustments and changes need to be made. Testing is an essential part of any solution, so you should get familiar with this window.

Finally, the main area of the screen is the editing canvas. Before you dive into customizing your bot, the interface presents a set of links to tutorials and supporting documentation. The **Get started** area talks about the three main task categories when working with bots, including the authoring, publishing, and monitoring of an agent, as seen here:

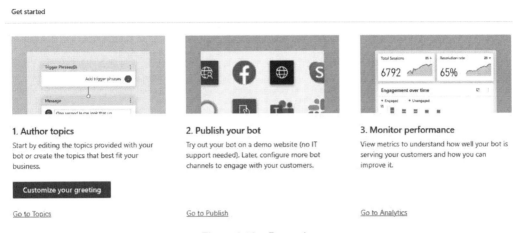

Figure 3.13 – Bot actions

Let's delve next into an example of creating and editing our first PVA.

Creating a Power Virtual Agent

We could start editing the current **MyFirstBot** agent; however, what we want to do is understand how to work with multiple bots in the same environment. We use a design involving multiple bots when we want to pass the conversation from one bot to another and each serves a distinct function. For example, we could have a bot handling billing inquiries, while another handles generic account updates. We do not want both of those functional conversations defined in the same bot as it will be harder to maintain in the future. For that reason, let's leave **MyFirstBot** as it is and create a brand-new bot:

1. Click the little robot icon at the top right of the page, as shown here:

Figure 3.14 – Action buttons

2. Find the **New bot** button and click it.

3. You are now presented with a wizard that collects several important pieces of information about your new bot. Give it a name, such as Hello there, and select a default language. In the **Environment** dropdown, select the environment where you want this bot to live or create a new one. The following screenshot shows this wizard window:

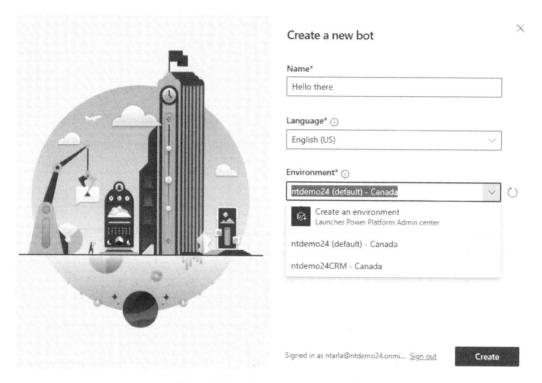

Figure 3.15 – Create a new bot wizard

4. When done here, click on the **Create** button. After a few minutes of processing, the screen refreshes and you are now in the editing canvas for your new bot.

You can go to the **Bots** navigation at the top right of the screen and you will now see the two bots. The current one is checked, and selecting the other takes you back to the editor for the first bot.

Let's see what our **Hello there** bot does out of the box and then make some small tweaks:

1. If the **Test bot** window is not expanded by default, click on the **Test your bot** button to display it.

2. In the message area at the bottom, type in Hello. After a few moments, the bot will respond as shown in the following screenshot:

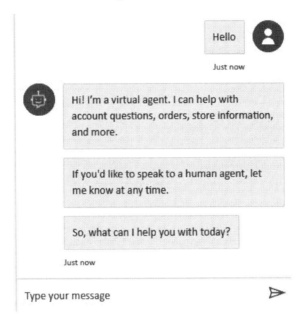

Figure 3.16 – Bot conversation

Look at that! We did not have to do anything, and our new agent is talking to us. Isn't that cool?

Now let's see the default functionality provided, as well as why and how this happens based on the configuration of this default bot.

On the left navigation area, select the **Topics** tab. Topics are definitions for the conversation the agent will have with the people interacting with it. They are nothing more than templates for how a conversation will play out.

As soon as you select **Topics**, the editing canvas changes to present a list of predefined topics:

+ New topic   📝 Suggest topics

Topics ⓘ

Existing (12)   Suggested (0)

Type	Name	Trigger phrases	Status
💬	Lesson 1 - A simple topic	(4) When are you closed	⬤ On
💬	Lesson 2 - A simple topic with a condition and variable	(5) Are there any stores aroun...	⬤ On
💬	Lesson 3 - A topic with a condition, variables and a pre-built ...	(5) Buy items	⬤ On
💬	Lesson 4 - A topic with a condition, variables and custom en...	(5) What is the best product f...	⬤ On
🗨	Greeting	(52) Good afternoon	Always on
🗨	Escalate	(65) Talk to agent	Always on
🗨	End of Conversation	No trigger phrases	Always on
🗨	Confirmed Success	No trigger phrases	Always on
🗨	Confirmed Failure	No trigger phrases	Always on
🗨	Goodbye	(67) Bye	Always on
🗨	Start over	(3) start over	Always on
🗨	Thank you	(4) thanks	Always on

Figure 3.17 – Bot topics

As you can see, a list of predefined topics is already added to our agent definition. These can serve as a starting point for our definition, where we can modify or remove them as needed. **Lessons 1** through to **4** are detailed examples to help you understand various concepts, while the remaining ones are default system topics that will exist with all agents. They handle generic expected behaviors, such as greetings for conversation starters, conversation end scenarios, as well as failures, and cannot be removed.

Returning to our agent conversation, we are greeted with the word **Hello**. This triggered an action from the agent based on one of the defined topics. If we open up the **Greeting** topic, we are presented with a list of trigger phrases, as seen in the following screenshot:

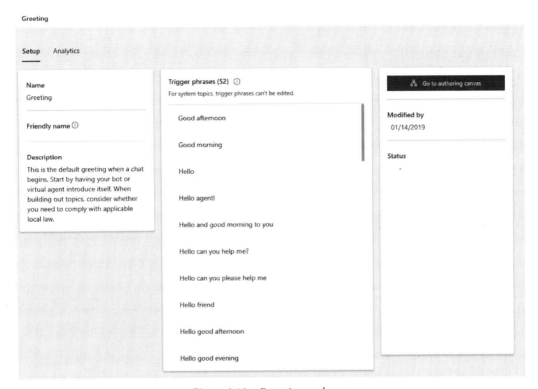

Figure 3.18 – Bot trigger phrases

Here, we can see that we have a total of 52 possible keywords that would trigger this conversation, and **Hello** is one of them.

Select **Go to authoring canvas** to see the details of the expected agent behavior. The following screenshot shows this definition:

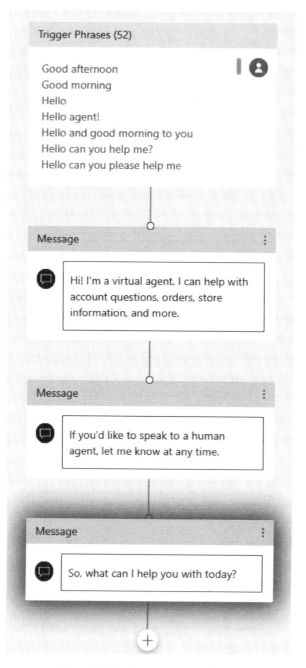

Figure 3.19 – Bot conversation flow

The agent responds to our greeting with three distinct messages. These are the exact messages that we have seen in the conversation window.

Let's add a new message by selecting the plus (+) sign at the bottom of the bot editing flow diagram. This presents us with a selection of possible actions we can define:

Figure 3.20 – Modifying the bot conversation

Because we intend to simply add another message, let's select the **Show a message** option. We will review the other choices throughout the book as we start to create more complex scenarios later on. The following screenshot shows the result of our selection:

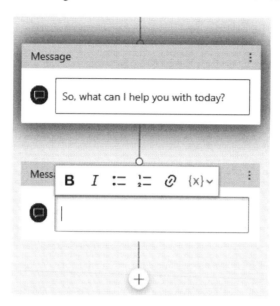

Figure 3.21 – Add a new message

As you can see, we can add a new message, and we also have some basic formatting options. We can create simple text messages, format some of the text in bold or as a list, add a link, or drop in a variable. We will learn more about variables as we see other examples. For now, let's simply add a **Hello, World!** message and save.

Returning to the test window, let's greet our agent with **Hello** again. The result will include the newly added message at the bottom, as shown here:

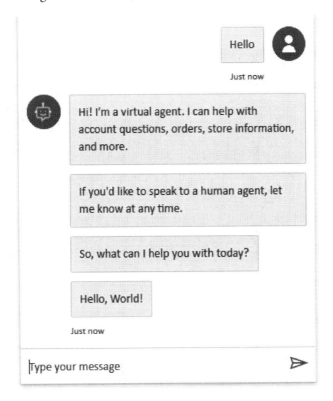

Figure 3.22 – Updated conversation

If you still have the **Topic authoring canvas** open, you will also see this execution, as well as a green check for each of the steps that were successfully executed:

Figure 3.23 – Conversation steps completed successfully

Now you can give yourself a pat on the back. You have just created, modified, and executed your very first PVA bot. Congratulations! Let's look next at how to publish our bot to all users.

Publishing a Power Virtual Agent

Once we are satisfied with the behavior of our agent, and the testing was successful, there is one more step required before we can make it available to the world: we need to publish it. Let's see how to do that:

1. Select the **Publish** option in the navigation bar on the left side of the screen.

2. This presents an editing canvas with a **Publish** button, along with some additional learning topics. Select the **Publish** button, as shown here:

Figure 3.24 – Bot publish

3. On the confirmation popup, select **Publish** again.

To see how our agent will look in a real-life scenario, under the **Share your bot** area, select the link to the demo website. Type Hello again and observe the modified response as expected.

That is great. We have now created a bot, slightly tweaked its functionality, and published it for users to start leveraging. We made some great progress.

Summary

Congratulations, you are now a bot author! You just took your first step on the path to knowledge.

Throughout this chapter, we learned how to create our trial environment and how to create our first PVA bot. While our agent does a few things "out of the box," we learned how to extend it by adding a new message to the response. Finally, we learned that we need to publish our bot to make it available for the masses.

In the next chapter, we will continue by tackling a slightly more complex scenario. We will build on top of the knowledge gained so far and make our agent smarter, by implementing some decision logic, as well as guiding the user through possible expected answers.

Section 2: Leveraging Power Virtual Agents on Your Website

In this section, you will learn about the process of creating and surfacing a Power Virtual Agent on your public site. Some common scenarios will be covered, as described by each chapter.

This section contains the following chapters:

- *Chapter 4, Creating a Power Virtual Agent for Your Website*
- *Chapter 5, Integrating a Power Virtual Agent into Your Website*
- *Chapter 6, Handling Authentication and Personalization*

4
Creating a Power Virtual Agent for Your Website

In the last chapter, we built our first basic **Power Virtual Agent** (**PVA**). To continue from there, let's see how we can infuse some real business logic into it.

As we saw in *Chapter 3, Building Your First Power Virtual Agent Chatbot*, a lot of functionality is already available with the creation of a new PVA. This serves to provide enough logic to be able to run the agent and interact with it, but it is not necessarily what the business expects to see as far as functionality. We will look at that in this chapter.

The chapter will focus on the following topics:

- Introducing a PVA for your website

- Description of the business scenario

- Extending our basic PVA

- A look at decision logic

- Guiding the conversation

At the end of this chapter, we will have built our first business requirements-driven PVA. We will see how we can map a real-world scenario requested by the business to the technology, and the output will look and behave more realistically.

Let's get started!

Introducing a PVA for your website

As we saw in the previous chapter, we have an extremely basic agent in place. It handles by default some basic conversation, but it does not really do anything useful for a business.

The provided default functionality handles basic System Topics, as described in the next sections.

The Greeting Topic

This Topic is the first **System Topic** we will look at. It allows the bot to be triggered by a greeting, and we have a total of 52 default greeting messages in the default language. These cannot be adjusted, modified, or removed. The **Greeting Topic** is included with all bots and cannot be disabled.

The default functionality is handling the predefined trigger words or phrases, and simply responds with a greeting and the default "how can I help you?" question:

Figure 4.1 – The Greeting Topic

This is your typical entry point into a new conversation with a virtual agent. You can choose to modify the default responses, and some organizations choose to personalize the conversation by providing an actual name for the virtual agent.

The Thank you Topic

This is another default System Topic and is included with all bots. It cannot be removed, but the response can be adjusted as needed.

This is triggered by four default words or phrases and only provides a simple message in response:

Figure 4.2 – The Thank you Topic

The Start over Topic

Another non-removable System Topic, the **Start over** Topic allows a conversation to be restarted or reset. It is triggered by three different trigger words or phrases, and it follows a similar linear pattern, with an added redirect at the end to the **Greeting Topic**, as shown in the following screenshot:

Figure 4.3 – The Start over Topic

Observe how now we have a new piece of functionality available in the shape of a **Redirect** action. This action forwards the flow to another **Topic**. We will see later in the chapter how this can be introduced in a more comprehensive scenario.

The Goodbye Topic

Similar to the first few System Topics presented, this is another System Topic included by default and it cannot be removed. It is a linear topic, with a simple set of 67 default trigger words or phrases, and a simple response.

The Escalate Topic

This is another System Topic that must be present. This topic handles passing the conversation from the automated chatbot to a human. Now we start to see some more features, where the default 65 provided trigger words or phrases lead to a response with a link to start an interaction with a real person. The link is not filled in by default, and it will depend on the backend system used to continue the conversation with a real person.

The End of Conversation Topic

This is another System Topic present in all virtual agents, but here's where things start to get a little more interesting from a functionality perspective.

First off, this Topic is not activated by a set of triggers, as we have seen so far. Instead, this Topic will be called from another topic. As such, there is no need to declare any **Trigger Phrases**.

In addition, in this Topic we pose a question to the user, we capture the response in a variable, and we perform a conditional check on it. The following screenshot shows the definition of this Topic:

Figure 4.4 – The End of Conversation Topic

Finally, based on the satisfaction of specific conditions, we either forward the user to other Topics or we have the right-most branch, which we can customize to fit our business requirements.

We will build these conditional branches once we start building our custom bot in the section titled *A look at decision logic*.

The Confirmed Success Topic

This System Topic is again triggered only from another Topic and does not include any **Trigger Phrases**. If we look at the functionality provided, it starts by collecting a rating from the user in the form of star ratings, as shown in the following screenshot:

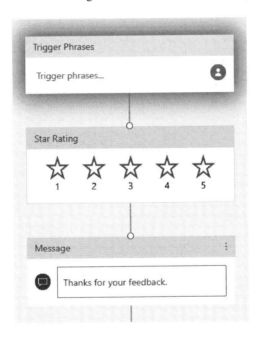

Figure 4.5 – The Confirmed Success Topic

It then goes on to ask whether additional help is required, captures the response, and decides how to proceed based on that response. The following screenshot shows the logic presented:

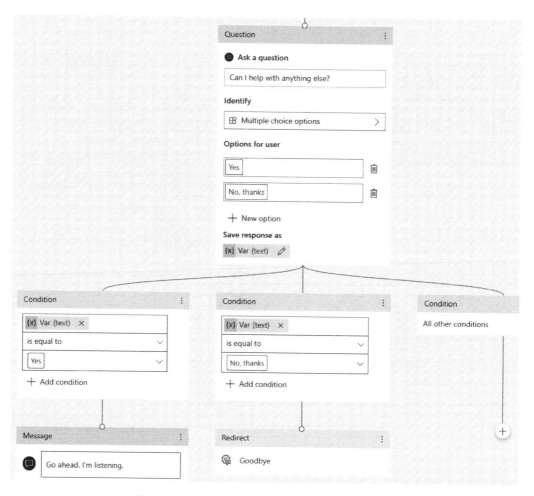

Figure 4.6 – Conditional decision-making in a Topic

A distinct difference to remark includes the ability to guide the user conversation by providing specific predefined answers to be selected. We will find out more about how to build this functionality in the section titled *Guiding the conversation* later in this chapter.

The Confirmed Failure Topic

The last System Topic provided is the **Confirmed Failure** Topic. This topic follows a similar pattern to the **Confirmed Success** Topic but handles the opposite scenario. From a functionality perspective, it does provide a question. It guides the user with standard predefined responses and applies conditional logic based on those responses. The following screenshot shows the definition of this Topic:

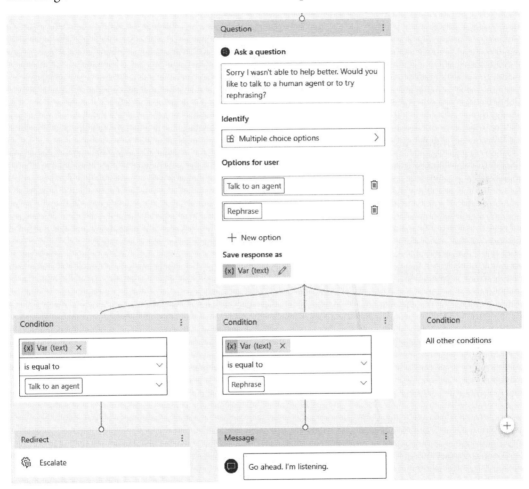

Figure 4.7 – The Confirmed Failure Topic

This concludes the list of System Topics available with any new PVA. But in addition to these System Topics, all new bots come with a set of **user topics** in the form of **Lessons**, as shown in the following screenshot:

Type	Name	Trigger phrases	Status
💬	Lesson 1 - A simple topic	(4) When are you closed	⬤ On
💬	Lesson 2 - A simple topic with a condition and variable	(5) Are there any stores aroun...	⬤ On
💬	Lesson 3 - A topic with a condition, variables and a pre-built ...	(5) Buy items	⬤ On
💬	Lesson 4 - A topic with a condition, variables and custom en...	(5) What is the best product f...	⬤ On

Figure 4.8 – The Lesson Topics

These Topics can be disabled altogether or can be fully modified and customized. They serve as learning materials, and anyone starting on the path of customizing PVAs should at the very least browse through these definitions to understand the available functionality.

Now that we understand the components making up a virtual agent, let's look at a more realistic business scenario.

Description of the business scenario

In this first business-inspired scenario, we will be looking at creating a conversation flow to capture requests for either account or technical support.

We will look at the following functional aspects of the creation process:

- Making a decision based on a user input
- Guiding a user through a specific set of choices

We want to first determine whether the user interacting with our virtual agent needs technical support regarding one of our products, or whether this is an account issue.

We will handle each of these separate scenarios through different Topics that will be triggered from a parent decision-making Topic.

Let's get started.

Extending our basic PVA

At this point, I am assuming you have created your basic virtual agent as described in *Chapter 3*, *Building Your First Power Virtual Agent Chatbot*. If you have not done so yet, just go to your environment and create a brand-new agent. You can reach the environment at https://powerva.microsoft.com.

In the **Topics** area, disable the four **user topics** that are provided by default as lessons. Your screen should look like this:

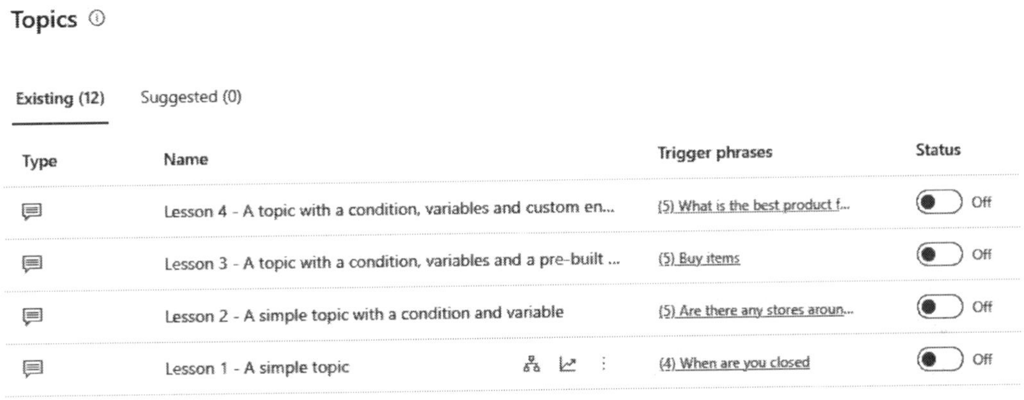

Topics ⓘ

Type	Name		Trigger phrases	Status
💬	Lesson 4 - A topic with a condition, variables and custom en...		(5) What is the best product f...	(●) Off
💬	Lesson 3 - A topic with a condition, variables and a pre-built ...		(5) Buy items	(●) Off
💬	Lesson 2 - A simple topic with a condition and variable		(5) Are there any stores aroun...	(●) Off
💬	Lesson 1 - A simple topic	🔗 〰 ⋮	(4) When are you closed	(●) Off

Existing (12)   Suggested (0)

Figure 4.9 – Topics disabled

Note that **Status** should be **Off** for all the **user topics**.

Next, let's create a new Topic. This Topic will handle the initial decision-making and sort the separate flows into either technical or account support. Let's follow these steps:

1. From the top ribbon, select the **New topic** option.

2. In the Topic definition, provide at a minimum a **Name** for this Topic. We will name ours in this example `Support decision`, as shown in the following screenshot:

Figure 4.10 – Creating a New topic

3. Make sure to click **Save topic** once you have it defined. We will be triggering this Topic right after the greeting and will not require any trigger phrases.

4. In order to wire it up after the **Greeting Topic**, select **Topics** from the left navigation and find **Greeting Topic**. Select **Go to authoring canvas** to make the necessary changes to the **Greeting Topic**.

5. Delete the last default message in the **Greeting Topic** and add a **Go to another topic** action, as shown in the following screenshot:

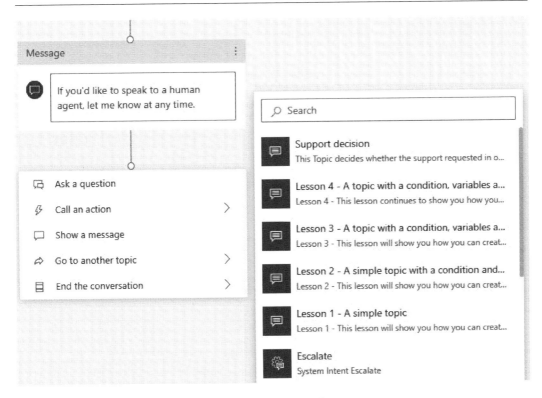

Figure 4.11 – Going to another topic

6. In the popup that appears on the right, select the Topic we just created, namely the **Support decision** Topic.

7. Make sure to select the **Save** option in the top-right corner of the ribbon. You can also check the Topic for errors by selecting the **Topic checker** button, as shown in the next screenshot:

Figure 4.12 – Topic checker on the ribbon

8. Now return to the **Support decision** topic editing canvas. You will see **Topic checker** lighting up with a red bubble, indicating this Topic is incomplete or incorrect, and the first message box is highlighted.

Let's see in the next section how to make decisions based on a user's response.

A look at decision logic

In order to make a decision, let's add a question for the user. In the **Support decision** Topic, delete the default message and select the + icon to add a question instead. We will ask whether the support request is related to a technical issue or an account issue. It should look like the following screenshot:

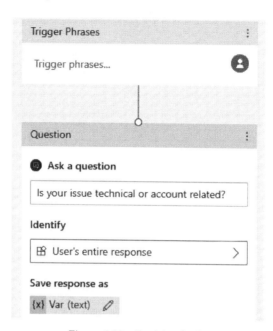

Figure 4.13 – Decision logic

Next, select the + sign and add a condition. Configure it as shown in the following screenshot:

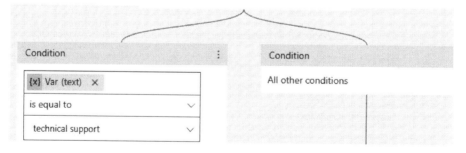

Figure 4.14 – Condition handling

On the **All other conditions** branch, we assume that this is not a technical support issue and we want to connect the user to a real live agent for account support. We can configure it by adding a message, followed by a redirect action to the **Escalate Topic**. The following screenshot shows this configuration:

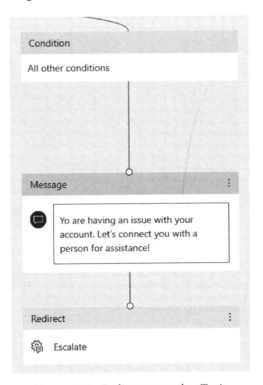

Figure 4.15 – Redirect to another Topic

If the customer's issue is a technical support issue, we can start drilling down into more details to narrow down the scope and try to provide the necessary support.

Let's test the scenario we've built so far. In the bot testing area, type `Hello` to trigger a new conversation. As you converse with the bot, the Topic editing canvas will reflect the stage the conversation is at, as well as the path it follows. The following screenshot shows the conversation guided to the escalation:

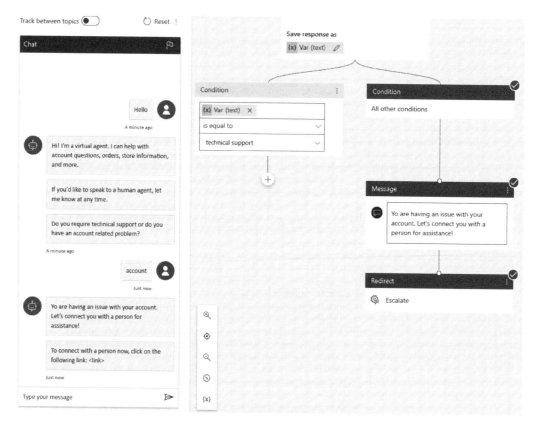

Figure 4.16 – Validating execution

Make sure you save your work so far. In the following section, we will tackle technical support by showing how to guide the user with pre-selected options rather than letting them input the information.

Guiding the conversation

As we have seen so far, we can capture the user input and make a decision based on it. But that can be error-prone, as the user could mistype or type something unexpected, which would take it to the **All other conditions** branch.

A better way, when possible, is to provide a preset group of responses to the user. This not only makes it easier for us to handle scenarios but also makes it easier for the user, who does not have to type anything now. You could create a final branch to handle all other conditions, but you will not be able to be as specific. This is when you might want to either escalate or ask additional questions.

Let's see how we do that.

In the **Support decision** topic, find the original **Condition** where we are expecting the user to type technical support. We will leave that as is but will try to narrow down the type of support needed while providing a set of standard responses.

Select **Ask a question** on that condition branch. We want to see whether this is a technical issue with a purchased product, a request for assistance with configuration, or another type of technical issue. So, our question could be as shown in the following screenshot:

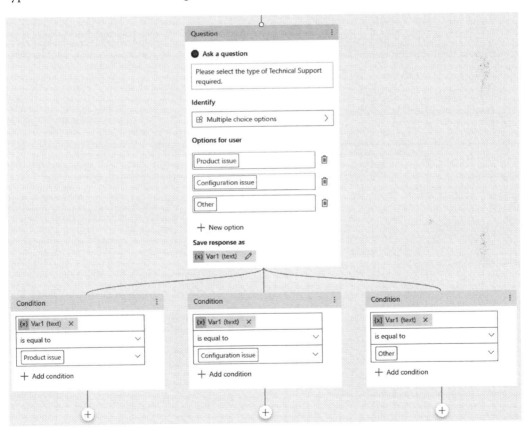

Figure 4.17 – Guiding the user conversation with predefined answers

As you can see, for each response option you add, a new **Condition** branch is created. You can also have several conditions grouped together. Let's assume that for both **Product issue** and **Other** we will redirect to a live person for support. We could configure the first condition to cover both scenarios, as shown in the following screenshot:

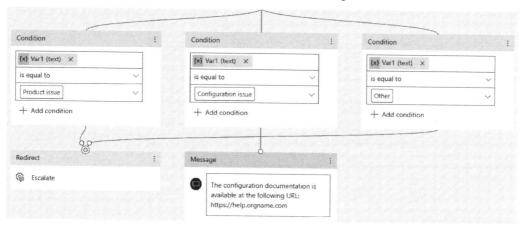

Figure 4.18 – Handling conditions

For the remaining condition, we can display a message to the user, then confirm that this was indeed helpful. We do this as shown in *Figure 4.19*:

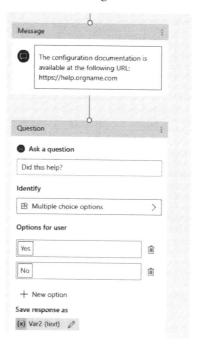

Figure 4.19 – Follow-up question

Finally, since this generates another set of conditions, we want to thank the user and end the conversation if they are satisfied or restart the process if not. We achieve this with the configuration shown in the following screenshot:

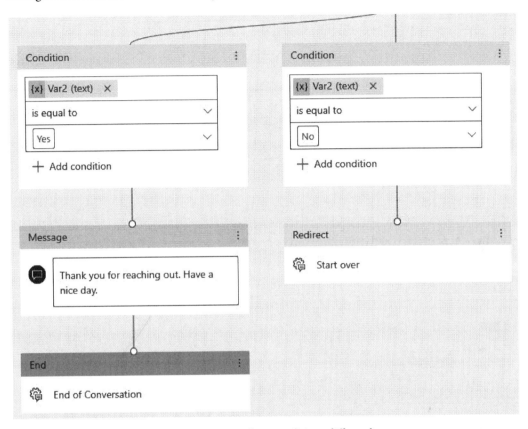

Figure 4.20 – Handling conditions differently

Great! Now all that is left is to try this scenario. If you closed the bot testing window to make more room on the editing canvas, re-open it by clicking on the **Test your bot** button and trigger a new conversation by typing in a greeting. Track through the conversation's steps and validate that the expected behavior is presented. The following screenshot shows this process tracked through to the end:

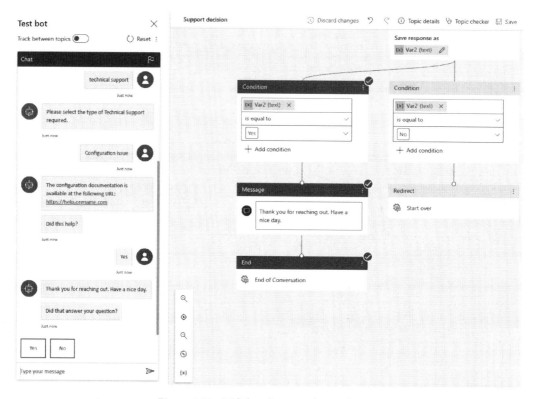

Figure 4.21 – Validate functionality and test

Try all the possible paths through the conversation and make sure the expected behavior is reflected. The presented visuals will reflect all the different paths, and it will be really easy to determine if you have missed one.

As we have seen so far, we can create new behaviors for our bots through the use of custom Topics, we can relate and transition from one topic to another, we can make decisions based on the response provided by the user, or we can guide the user through the path with standard predefined responses.

Summary

Congratulations, you are now a bot author! You just took your first step on the path to knowledge.

Throughout this chapter, we learned how to create our trial environment and how to create our first PVA bot. While our agent does a few things out of the box, we learned how to extend it by adding a new message to the response.

Finally, we learned that we need to publish our bot to make it available for the masses.

In the next chapter, we will continue by tackling a slightly more complex scenario. We will build on the knowledge gained so far and make our agent smarter.

5

Integrating a Power Virtual Agent into Your Website

In previous chapters, we learned the basics of creating a functional **Power Virtual Agent (PVA)**, as well as how to track progress through its different logic branches. The final step is to have it published for customers or users to take advantage of it.

Continuing with the agent we created in the previous chapter, we will now look at how this can be integrated into a real website. When presenting this functionality to users, the most common way is to integrate this functionality into our organization's public website. We can choose to do this on a support page, on all the site pages, or only in specific areas of the site. This is a business decision that typically results from site traffic analysis along with the specific site structure.

In this chapter, we will focus on publishing our newly created bot to a website. We will look at the following topics:

- Testing the agent in the default demo website

- Where can we introduce a Power Virtual Agent?

- How to present our Power Virtual Agent

- One Power Virtual Agent versus many

By the end of this chapter, we will have our previously created PVA integrated into a simple sample website. We will understand some of the presentation options, and the challenges and skills required to achieve this. We will also look at some considerations when designing our PVA strategy with regard to the separation of functionality over multiple bots in different areas of a site.

So, let's get going!

Testing the agent in the default demo website

Besides the ability to test an agent's functionality in the standard editing canvas for each topic, we can also see how this could look in a default demo website.

To be able to open our newly created bot in a demo website, we first need to publish it:

1. On the left navigation area, select the **Publish** option. This will take you to the following screen:

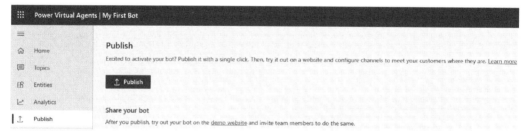

Figure 5.1 – Publishing a PVA

2. Select the **Publish** button on the presented screen and confirm the **Publish** option on the popup. This process will take a short while, after which you will get a message stating that the latest content has now been published. The following screenshot shows this confirmation message:

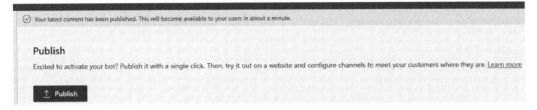

Figure 5.2 – Publishing confirmation

If you encounter any other warning messages, go back to the agent definition, find the topic that presents an error message, and select to edit the topic in the canvas.

> **Tip**
> Whenever you complete a topic, make sure to run the topic checker to make sure no errors are encountered.

3. Once your agent is published successfully, in the **Share your bot** section on the **Publish** page, find the demo website link, as shown in the following screenshot:

Figure 5.3 – Sharing a bot

4. Once you click on the demo website link, a new browser tab opens and the bot window is presented in the context of a web page. On the right side of the page, you will see a window with the bot name in the header, a conversation canvas, and a message box at the bottom. The following screenshot shows this page:

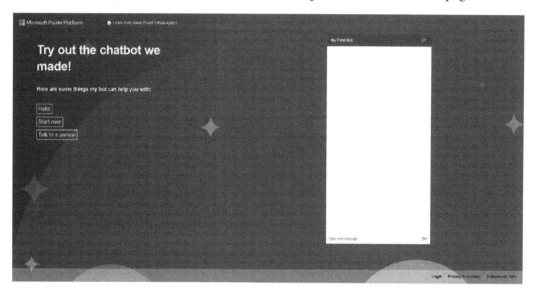

Figure 5.4 – Testing your bot in a demo website

5. You can test the same functionality we tested during the topic testing, and you should see the same behavior from the agent.

Opening the **Developer tools** browser, we can now look at the content of this page and how the bot is integrated.

We will find that the header is a `div` tag on its own with a class of `header-118`, while the actual bot functionality is within another `div` tag just below it, as seen in the following screenshot:

Figure 5.5 – HTML5 code

This is your standard HTML5 page structure definition, and you can tweak the look and feel as needed. Web design is not within the scope of this book, but if you need assistance in this regard, coordinate with your web design team for the presentation elements when integrating a PVA into a public website.

Now, you might ask, "What is the difference between testing the agent's functionality in the editing canvas versus in the demo website?" That would be an excellent question! After all, the functionality behind the scenes is the same.

The reason we can test this agent in a demo website is to enable other users in the organization, typically business users with no technical skills, to validate the fact that the agent is indeed behaving as needed. Once you have it published to the demo website, you can share the link to that page with your business users and collect their feedback and/or approval.

Let's see next where it makes sense to present our chatbot.

Where can we introduce a Power Virtual Agent?

Now that the agent has been published and business users are trying out its functionality, it is time to start thinking about its destination. We obviously built this to serve more than just a handful of testers.

As we have seen so far in this chapter, the agent can be deployed to a website. We will see in the second half of this book how an agent can be created and deployed within **Microsoft Teams**. As Microsoft Teams is becoming the central hub within an organization, we are encountering new scenarios where a virtual agent would be beneficial within our organization.

In addition, we can also consider integrating agents into a Facebook page or a mobile or custom application. For these scenarios, you should review the documentation provided by Microsoft at `https://docs.microsoft.com`.

Going back to our website as the end target destination, we can now start analyzing where it makes the most sense to have a virtual agent. A lot of organizations place an agent right on their front page, along with some or all of the other pages of the website. And that might be OK. But from a **User Experience (UX)** perspective, do you want every user hitting your main page only to be greeted with a "How may I help you?" message?

In addition, do you want the same agent functionality to be presented on all of the site's pages?

You might consider not placing an agent at all on the home page and having separate agents for the various areas of your site. For example, when a user navigates to the support area of your site, you might want to consider triggering a support agent. Alternatively, when a user navigates to the products or services area of your site, you could have another agent that focuses on narrowing the choices and forwarding the user to the exact service or product they are interested in.

Following the same logic, you can create and incorporate various agents for specific areas of your website.

From a presentation perspective, and this is a very design-focused approach, some organizations choose to animate the presentation, and attract the user's eyes toward the agent area. This could be beneficial, but it could also be a distraction for the user.

I would recommend having a design discussion with representatives from various aspects of your organization before making decisions. You might want to consult with a UX expert, along with a web designer and graphics designer, before a decision is made on how, where, and in what manner your agent will be presented to users.

Let's see next how to present our chatbot.

How to present our Power Virtual Agent

OK, so coming right after the discussion about UX and graphics design, this section does not focus on any of those topics. Those should be discussed with your organization experts and decided based on your organization's needs and standards. There is no *one template fits all* scenario here.

Rather than focusing on the visual aspect, I want to look at how we introduce our agent into a page. We are not going to look at visual presentation, or animations, or UX. Instead, we will only look at the plumbing needed to have the agent available on our website.

The current bot editor interface also guides us through this process. It is an almost no-code experience. Fine, we need to copy a snippet of code from one place to another, but really, we're not creating anything in code. No coding experience is necessary.

On the left-hand navigation of the bot editor interface, go to **Manage**, and then select **Channels**, as seen in the following screenshot:

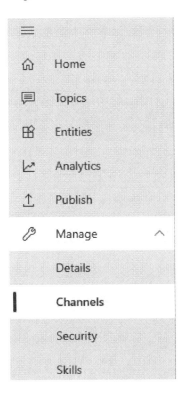

Figure 5.6 – Selecting an available presentation channel

Once you make the selection, you are presented with a list of available channels to present your newly created bot. This list will refresh with new channels as more are added. The following screenshot shows the current channels available:

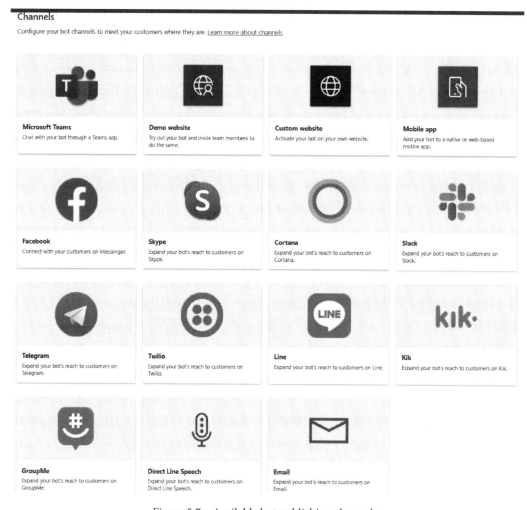

Figure 5.7 – Available bot publishing channels

As you can see, we have a number of channels available. For this section, we want to focus our attention on the **Custom website** option.

We will be looking at building and publishing bots for **Microsoft Teams** in the second half of this book. We have already seen the **Demo website** functionality. For all the other choices, you can refer to the Microsoft documentation available at `https://docs.microsoft.com`.

Once we select the **Custom website** option, we are presented with a slide-out section entitled **Custom website** that presents a link to the documentation, along with **Default embed code**. The page looks like the following screenshot:

Custom website   ×

This channel allows you to embed an HTML chatbot into your website. Learn about embedding your bot in a web page.

Default embed code

Copy the following code snippet and paste it to your HTML website. If you do not have access to the website's code, share the code with the person responsible for your website.

```
<!DOCTYPE html> <html> <body> <iframe src="https://powerva.microsoft.com/webchat/bots/e0454a78-cfa1-4be7-9b54-44294fdae4c0" frameborder="0" style="width: 100%; height: 100%;"> </iframe> </body> </html>
```

[Copy]   [Share to email]

Single sign-on embed code

Get a single sign-on enabled chat canvas to interact with your bot. Learn about single sign-on

Figure 5.8 – Getting the default embed code

Let's copy this code and then, in a text editor, let's create a basic HTML page and embed this code in it. Note that the code generated includes the entire HTML page definition.

Open a new document in Notepad and paste the copied code therein. Save the file on your desktop with a name such as `mybot.html` and then go to the location where you have saved it and double-click on it to open it in your browser.

After taking a moment to load, your page should refresh to display the most basic conversation window, as seen in the following screenshot:

Figure 5.9 – A basic web page bot

Note that there is minimal formatting and styling. You can test the functionality of your bot here also, and see that it will respond to the standard conversational topics we defined during the creation of our bot.

Opening the browser's **Developer tools** window again, you will find the exact code that we pasted, as indicated here:

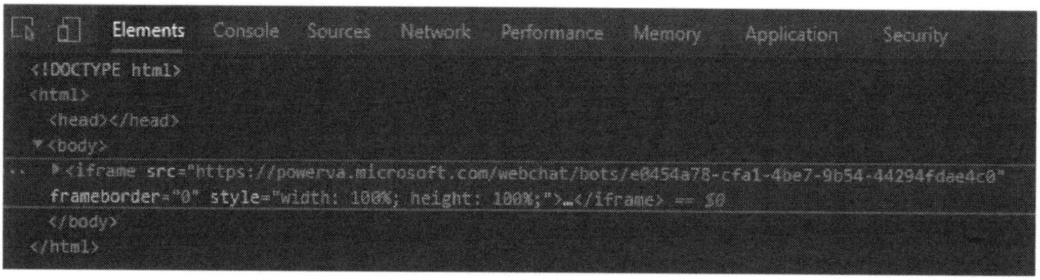

Figure 5.10 – Web page bot code

Expanding the `iframe` block will reveal other details on how this is automatically built. We do not need to delve into the nuts and bolts of the autogenerated code; just know that the main iframe is pointing to the bot you created, using the URL `https://powerva.microsoft.com/webchat/bots/` followed by the unique identifier of your bot.

Now, if we look at an actual production page that includes a chatbot, we will find a more comprehensive story. Typically, you will find a bot icon, be this a human face or a stylized robot, or any other symbol. Most pages leveraging bots will present these on the bottom-right side of the screen.

A script will usually trigger on the **on-click** event of that icon. That is, when you click that image, an action will be performed. That action will typically involve displaying the actual conversation window we already have on our web page.

To be clear, this is not something specific to Microsoft Power Virtual Agents, but rather a standard web development piece of functionality. The same approach is used by other providers of bot solutions, as seen in the following screenshot from IBM Watson Assistant, IBM's own version of its virtual agent offering:

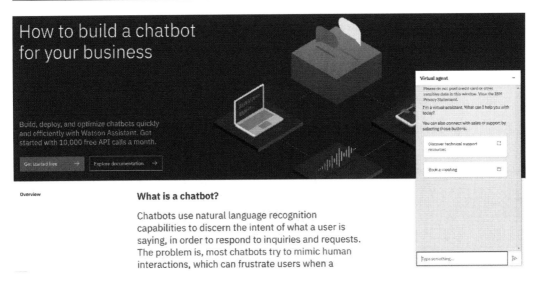

Figure 5.11 – IBM Watson Assistant

This is one example where the UX is actually quite similar to what we have seen so far with Microsoft Power Virtual Agents. Other sites take an even more graphical approach, with more animated presentations. One such example is the **MobileMonkey** website chatbot, which presents a simple small icon, as seen in the following screenshot:

Figure 5.12 – MobileMonkey chatbot collapsed

Once you click this icon, the entire bot window is presented, as seen in the following screenshot:

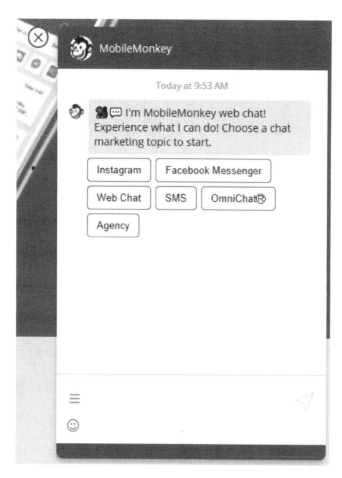

Figure 5.13 – MobileMonkey chat window expanded

This is a great example of maximizing the screen's real estate, with minimal intrusive behavior experience for the user. The larger chat window is only presented when requested by the user, but it is always available just a click away.

Finally, in the family of Power Platform applications, we have the Power Platform portal. We can easily integrate one of these chatbots into the portal by adding an **iframe** to a portal page and providing only the URL from the embedded code provided, as highlighted in the following screenshot:

Figure 5.14 – Providing the URL to an iframe

But let's look at the steps to achieve this:

1. If you do not have a Power Apps portal created in your tenant, you can create one by going to **Apps** in the **maker portal** and choosing to add a new app. This is done in a trial where you are a full admin, but in your environment, you must have the services and licenses necessary. Select **Portal**, follow the wizard steps to define the portal name and URL, and then wait for a few moments for the provisioning to take place. Your screen should look like the following screenshot while the portal is provisioning:

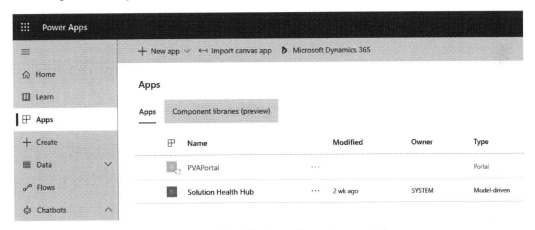

Figure 5.15 – Provisioning a Power Apps portal

2. Navigate to the **Portal editor** window by selecting **Portal App** and then choosing **Edit**. In the editor, select the **Three columns section** option on the main page and then, in the far-right column, choose to add an **IFrame** control. The choices displayed in the **Components** window are visible, as indicated in the following screenshot:

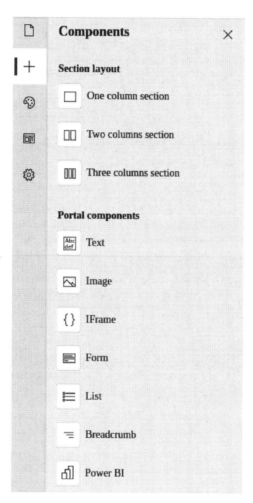

Figure 5.16 – Power portal editor components

3.   In the **IFrame** properties window, drop the URL selected in *Figure 5.14* earlier in the **Link** field. Your page will refresh to show the bot window, as seen here:

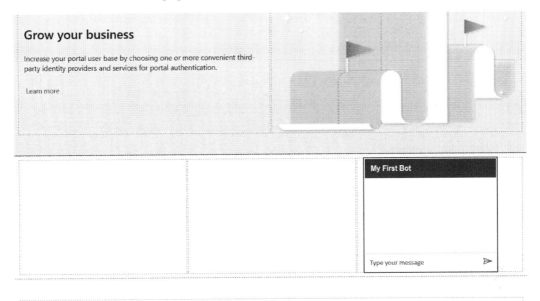

Figure 5.17 – Power Apps portal page with a chatbot inserted in IFrame

4. Clicking on the **Browse website** button in the top-right corner of the editor will open a new tab with the page including our bot, as shown in *Figure 5.18*:

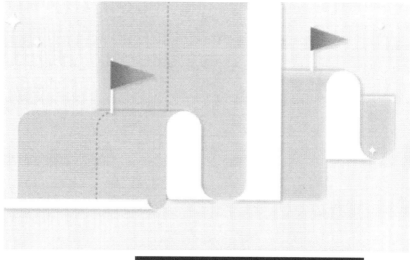

Figure 5.18 – Bot in a Power Apps portal page

5. You can now interact with your bot and confirm its functionality.

Again, you can style this as required, as well as choosing to drop it in another part or area of the page or pages of your portal.

By observing these approaches, we can easily integrate a chatbot into any public or private portal or website and provide full chatbot functionality to users.

Let's now look in the next section at a more efficient approach to structuring chatbots, and where it makes sense to create multiple agents versus cramming all the functionality into a single agent.

One Power Virtual Agent versus many

Typically, in an organization, you will start with one agent in a specific area of your website, serving a specific purpose. You will want to gauge the success, make improvements, and expand on that. Once you see the value, you will decide how to implement similar functionality across other areas of your site.

It is very seldom that a single bot will serve an entire site. Usually, you will structure the functionality based on the various functional areas of your public website. For example, in the **Support** area of your site, you will have a bot serving topics concerning user support. In the **Sales** area, you will have another bot serving more sales-focused topics, and so on.

Segmenting and separating the bot's functionality is beneficial from both a maintenance and support perspective, but also from the point of view of managing complexity, testability, and overall UX. After all, you do not want a bot to ask you whether your issue is sales- or service-related when you are already triggering it from the **Service** page.

The same way you design and define the various topics within a bot, you should consider a similar approach when deciding to split various bots according to their area of function. It is not uncommon to monitor a bot for a while and then decide that the customer would be better served by two separate functional bots. It is a continuous process of learning, adjusting, and monitoring. We are looking at a rinse and repeat process to achieve the best result.

Summary

Congratulations! You now have your first Power Virtual Agent published on a public website, and that is available for customers to use.

In this chapter, we looked at the default testing website, which provides basic functionality in the context of a sandbox website. From there, we took and published our bot to a sample website. We looked at where and how to integrate it into our site, along with some presentation considerations. We then introduced the same functionality to the Power Platform portal offering.

Finally, we closed this chapter with a discussion on strategy and how to design the PVA functionality to target various segments of our site.

In the next chapter, we will focus on a very important aspect of providing true customer support – the ability to authenticate users and provide personalized information.

6
Handling Authentication and Personalization

So far, we have looked at what **Power Virtual Agents** (**PVA**) is, the basics of how to license the service, how to build a basic bot with no code, the handling of some more complex scenarios, as well as integrating a bot into your current website. But all the examples we've looked at so far only targeted anonymous users, and no personalized information was provided. We are about to change that in this chapter.

In this chapter, we want to see how to recognize the user we are interacting with and provide a truly personalized experience. We will be looking at the following topics:

- Providing generalized information to users
- Providing a personalized experience to users
- Authentication considerations
- Leveraging various data sources

Along the way, we will learn how to configure standard authentication leveraging Azure AD, as well as how to get some basic user information by using Microsoft Graph.

At the end of this chapter, we will have a much more personalized virtual agent that can provide some basic personalized information to users. While this topic spans multiple authentication mechanisms and data sources, for the sake of simplicity, we will only look at the basics. This is an advanced topic and requires an understanding of some basic concepts around **Azure Active Directory** (**AAD**) configuration, authentication mechanisms and protocols, as well as the basics of Microsoft Graph. For all these topics and additional details, do consult the Microsoft documentation available at `docs.microsoft.com`.

And with all that being said, let's proceed.

Providing generalized information to users

In the previous chapters of this book, we looked at creating a simple chatbot and shaping a conversation with potential users. We saw how we can guide the conversation in a specific direction by either looking at the user input or providing predefined answers to enforce a certain conversation path.

To enhance the value of the information provided to users, we can also configure our bot to index our public website and provide information from a certain area, such as a **Frequently Asked Questions** (**FAQ**) section.

The configuration is relatively straightforward, as we will see next:

1. Open your existing configured bot or create a new one.

2. On the left navigation, select **Topics**, as seen in the following screenshot:

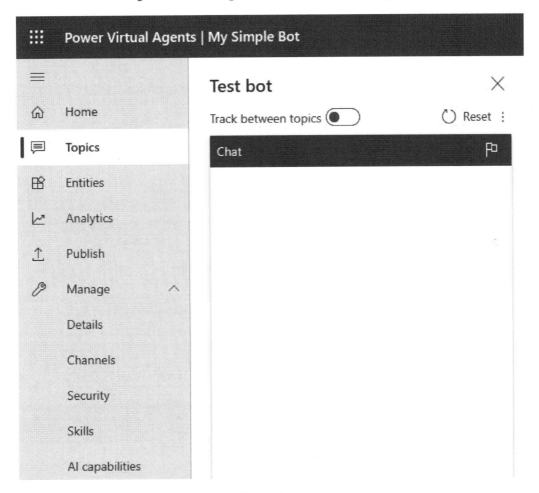

Figure 6.1 – PVA authoring navigation

3. On the **Topics** page, select the **Suggested** tab right under the page title, as shown in the following screenshot:

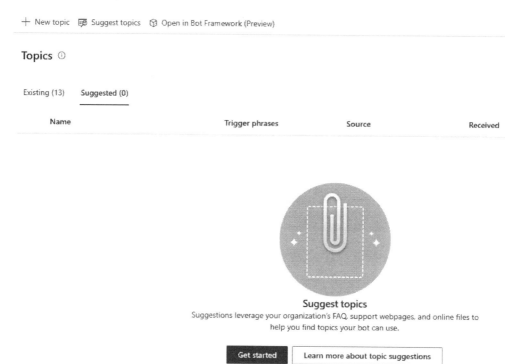

Figure 6.2 – Topics suggestions

4. If you have not used suggested topics before, select the **Get started** button.

5. On the following popup, provide a URL to the area to be indexed for information. Note that it must be a URL and must begin with `https://` as shown in the following screenshot:

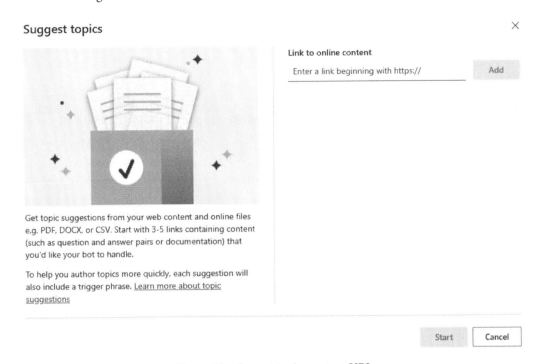

Figure 6.3 – Suggest topics content URL

6. Once you click on **Start**, the system processes the provided data source location and comes back with one or more suggested possible new **Topics**. The following screenshot shows the **Topics** suggested based on providing the URL to the following Microsoft Docs page: `https://docs.microsoft.com/en-us/power-virtual-agents/authoring-create-edit-topics`.

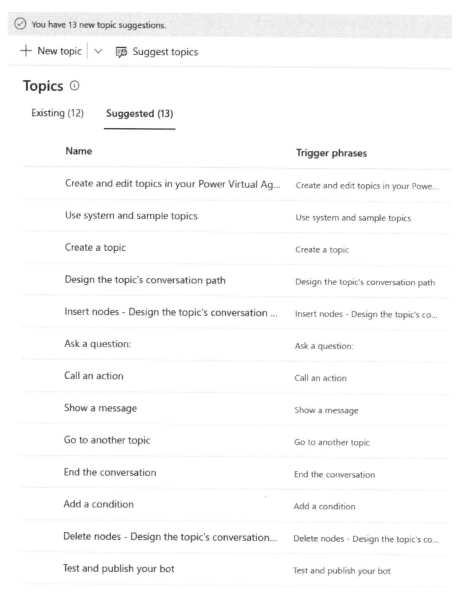

Figure 6.4 – Suggested topics list

7. Select the topics you want to add to your bot from the provided list, and on the top ribbon, select the option **Add to topics** as seen in the following screenshot:

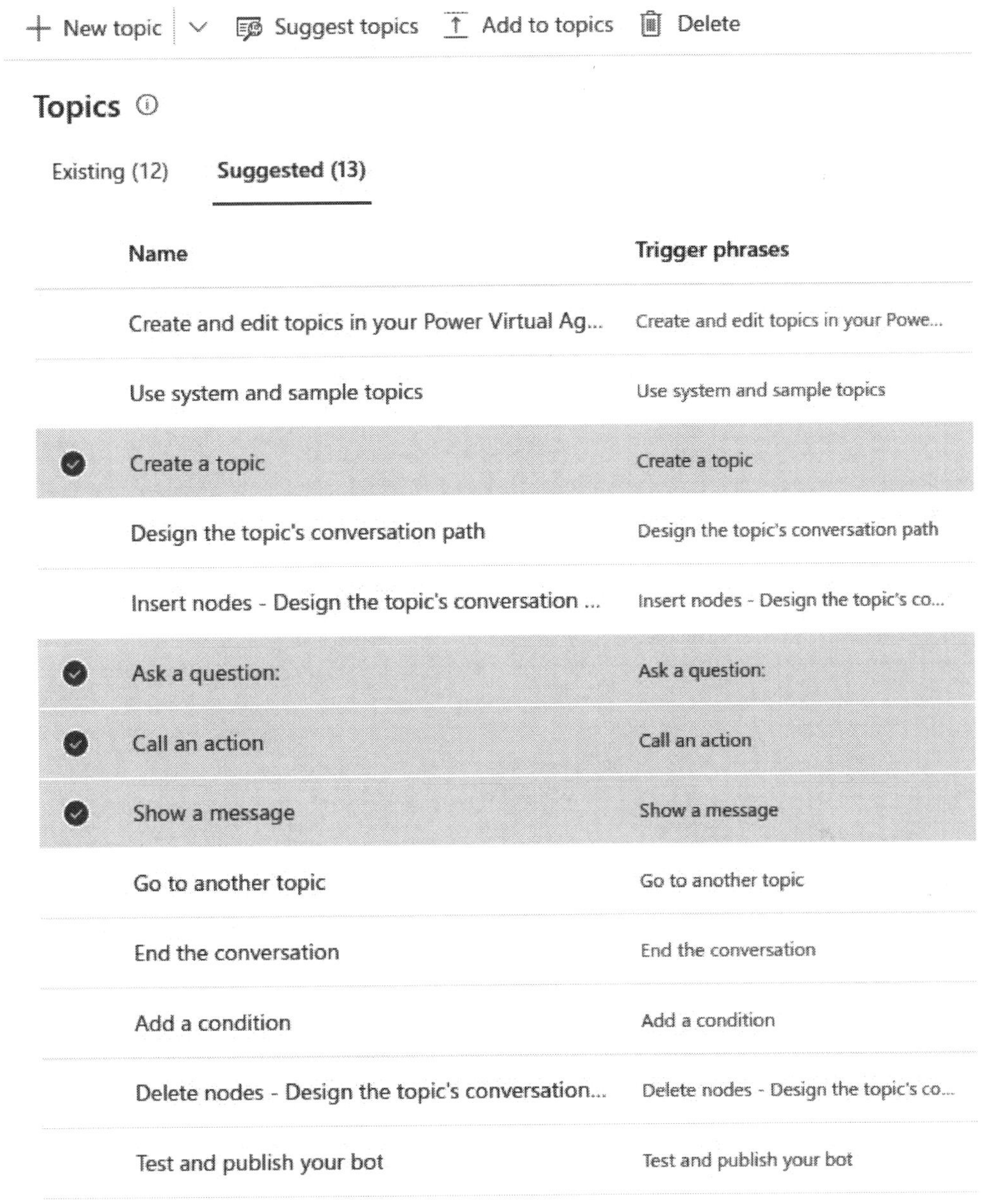

+ New topic ∨   📧 Suggest topics   ↑ Add to topics   🗑 Delete

Topics ⓘ

Existing (12)   **Suggested (13)**

Name	Trigger phrases
Create and edit topics in your Power Virtual Ag...	Create and edit topics in your Powe...
Use system and sample topics	Use system and sample topics
✓ Create a topic	Create a topic
Design the topic's conversation path	Design the topic's conversation path
Insert nodes - Design the topic's conversation ...	Insert nodes - Design the topic's co...
✓ Ask a question:	Ask a question:
✓ Call an action	Call an action
✓ Show a message	Show a message
Go to another topic	Go to another topic
End the conversation	End the conversation
Add a condition	Add a condition
Delete nodes - Design the topic's conversation...	Delete nodes - Design the topic's co...
Test and publish your bot	Test and publish your bot

Figure 6.5 – Adding the relevant Topics

8. You can click on any of the suggested topics to see the details, as shown in the following screenshot:

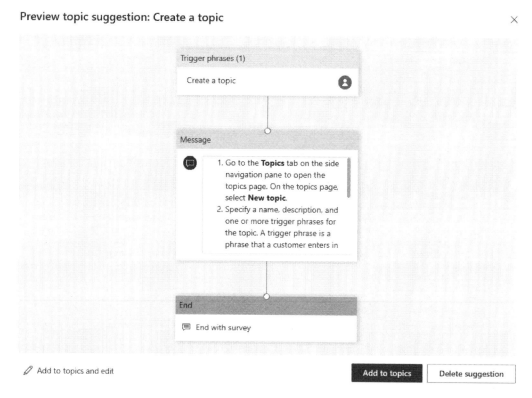

Figure 6.6 – Preview a suggested topic

9. Now that you have selected and added the suggested topics, you will find them in your list of existing topics. By default, they will be added in a disabled state, and you must enable them once you are satisfied with the configuration, as seen in the following screenshot:

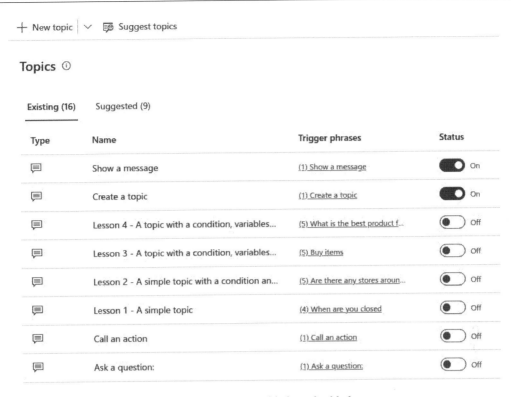

+ New topic ∨ 📑 Suggest topics

Topics ⓘ

Existing (16)   Suggested (9)

Type	Name	Trigger phrases	Status
💬	Show a message	(1) Show a message	⬤ On
💬	Create a topic	(1) Create a topic	⬤ On
💬	Lesson 4 - A topic with a condition, variables...	(5) What is the best product f...	◯ Off
💬	Lesson 3 - A topic with a condition, variables...	(5) Buy items	◯ Off
💬	Lesson 2 - A simple topic with a condition an...	(5) Are there any stores aroun...	◯ Off
💬	Lesson 1 - A simple topic	(4) When are you closed	◯ Off
💬	Call an action	(1) Call an action	◯ Off
💬	Ask a question:	(1) Ask a question:	◯ Off

Figure 6.7 – Topics added are disabled

10. With these topics created, you can now use them in the same manner that we leverage any other topics.

With these capabilities, we can now create complex content without having to type it in. We can leverage this capability to greatly enhance the ability of our agent to become *smarter* and *know* more about our business, products, services, or any other topics we choose as worthy of sharing with our users.

But what if we want to have a premium service, where we only provide this excellent service to a sub-set of paying customers? Let's look at personalized information next.

Providing a personalized experience to users

Great – so far, we've learned about creating non-personalized chatbots. But what if we need to determine who the user at the other end is?

Welcome to authentication. This is a slightly more complex topic. In this scenario, we will look at authenticating a user against **AAD**, as well as retrieving some basic information about the user from their Microsoft Graph profile.

There are, of course, more complex scenarios you might want to dabble in, but this topic should put you on the right path to understanding the basic concepts around authenticating users.

Let's now see what that's all about.

Working with authentication has been simplified as much as possible by Microsoft. For the most part, it's simply a matter of configuration and mapping the correct keys in the right place. But let's look at this:

1. Start by navigating to your existing chatbot. If you are starting fresh, create a new chatbot if one is not available.

2. On the left navigation, find and expand the **Manage** area, and locate the **Security** area underneath, as shown in the following screenshot:

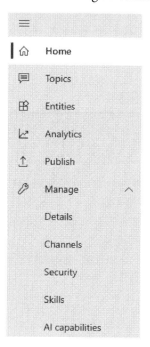

Figure 6.8 – Find Security in the menu

3. In the window that opens, find and select the **Authentication** section, as seen in the following screenshot:

Security

Set up additional security measures for the bot and your users.

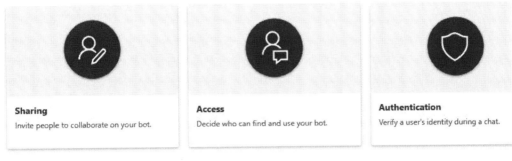

Figure 6.9 – Finding the Authentication area

4. Once you select **Authentication**, you are provided with a selection for the type of authentication you are configuring, as seen in the next screenshot:

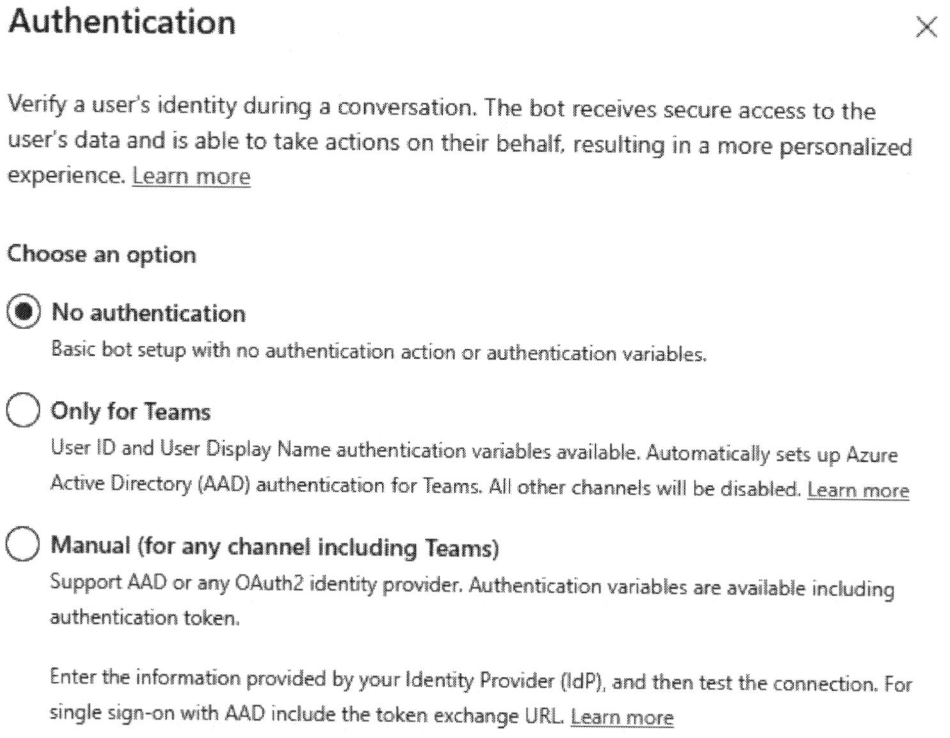

Authentication   ✕

Verify a user's identity during a conversation. The bot receives secure access to the user's data and is able to take actions on their behalf, resulting in a more personalized experience. Learn more

Choose an option

⦿ **No authentication**
Basic bot setup with no authentication action or authentication variables.

◯ **Only for Teams**
User ID and User Display Name authentication variables available. Automatically sets up Azure Active Directory (AAD) authentication for Teams. All other channels will be disabled. Learn more

◯ **Manual (for any channel including Teams)**
Support AAD or any OAuth2 identity provider. Authentication variables are available including authentication token.

Enter the information provided by your Identity Provider (IdP), and then test the connection. For single sign-on with AAD include the token exchange URL. Learn more

Figure 6.10 – Select the Authentication type

5. Obviously, for our scenario, we want to look at authenticating public users. The first choice provided is the default, **No authentication**. The second option allows us to authenticate when creating a virtual agent for Teams. We will cover that in *Chapter 8, Integrating the Power Virtual Agent into Teams*. For the purpose of this scenario, we are looking at the **Manual** option. Select that third option and you will be presented with additional configuration, as shown in the following screenshot:

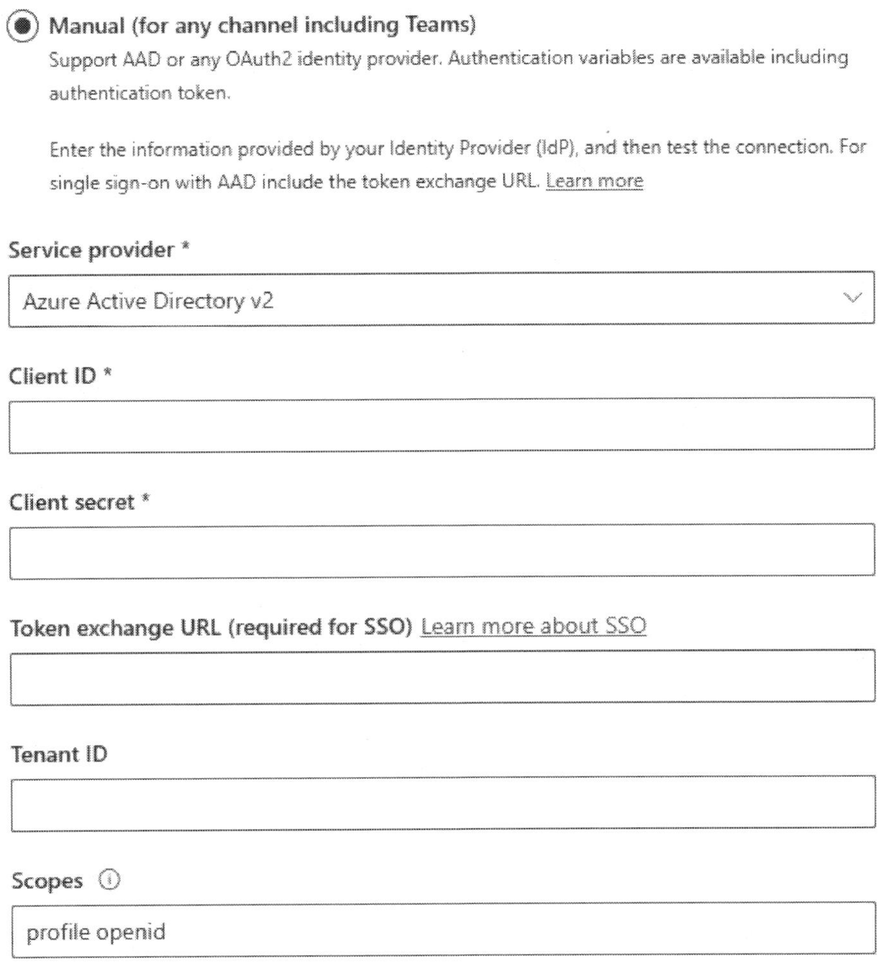

⊙ **Manual (for any channel including Teams)**

Support AAD or any OAuth2 identity provider. Authentication variables are available including authentication token.

Enter the information provided by your Identity Provider (IdP), and then test the connection. For single sign-on with AAD include the token exchange URL. Learn more

Service provider *

| Azure Active Directory v2 | ⌄ |

Client ID *

Client secret *

Token exchange URL (required for SSO) Learn more about SSO

Tenant ID

Scopes ⓘ

profile openid

Figure 6.11 – Authentication configuration

6. Looking at **Service provider**, we can choose between **Azure Active Directory (AAD)**, **Azure Active Directory v2** or **Generic OAauth 2**. This allows flexibility in configuration, by providing support not only for Microsoft's standard AAD but also any generic identity provider supporting the standard **OAuth 2**. Let's stick in this example to Microsoft's AAD setup.

7. At this point, we need to perform a little bit of configuration on the Azure Active Directory side. Navigate in a new tab or browser window to `portal.azure.com` and log in with a global admin account.

8. Once logged in, find and go to the **App registrations** area.

9. Create a new **App registration**, as seen in the following screenshot:

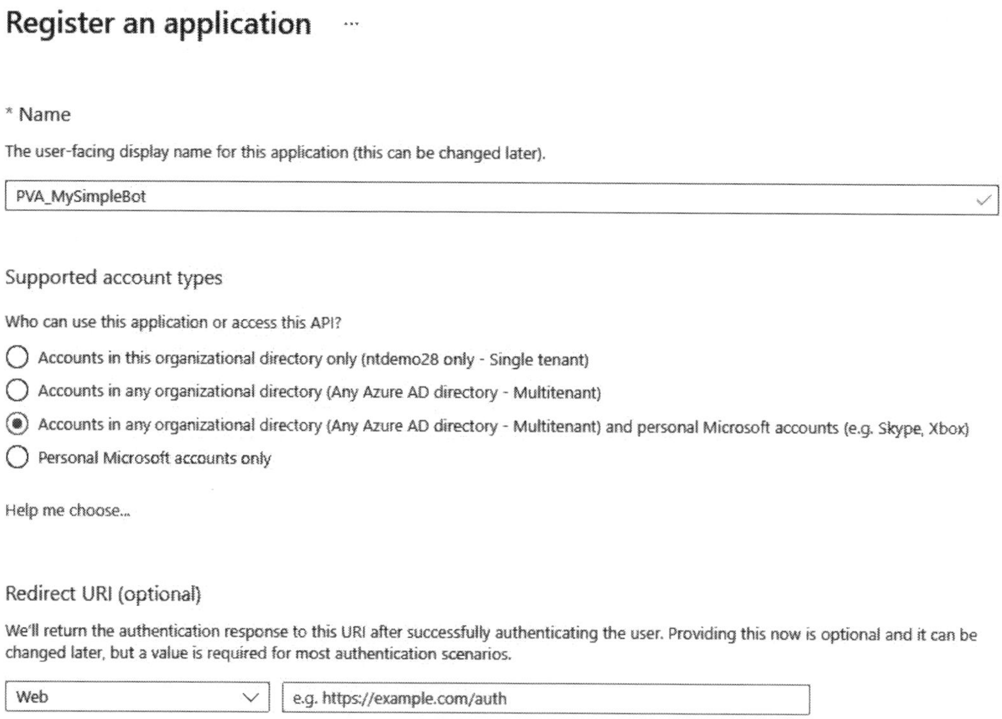

Register an application   ⋯

* Name

The user-facing display name for this application (this can be changed later).

PVA_MySimpleBot	✓

Supported account types

Who can use this application or access this API?

○ Accounts in this organizational directory only (ntdemo28 only - Single tenant)

○ Accounts in any organizational directory (Any Azure AD directory - Multitenant)

◉ Accounts in any organizational directory (Any Azure AD directory - Multitenant) and personal Microsoft accounts (e.g. Skype, Xbox)

○ Personal Microsoft accounts only

Help me choose...

Redirect URI (optional)

We'll return the authentication response to this URI after successfully authenticating the user. Providing this now is optional and it can be changed later, but a value is required for most authentication scenarios.

Web ∨	e.g. https://example.com/auth

Figure 6.12 – Register a new application in AAD

10. Select the option for both accounts within an **AAD tenant** as well as **personal Microsoft accounts**. This will allow both organization and public users with a standard Microsoft account to log in.

11. Once done, click on the **Register** button. You are presented next with a window with details about the application registered, as seen in the following screenshot:

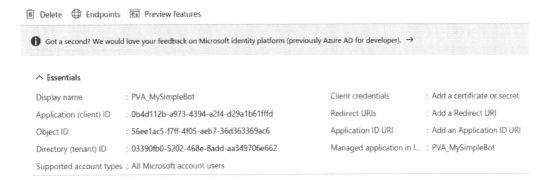

Figure 6.13 – App registration details

12. Take note of the presented details, as we will require these in the configuration. The screenshot is from a trial environment that will not be available by the time this title is published, so there is no need to protect the presented IDs.

13. We can quickly see that the client ID, **Application (client) ID**, is readily available, and we can grab it and populate it in the chatbot authentication configuration area. We can also grab the **Directory (tenant) ID** and use it to populate the **Tenant ID** field on the chatbot authentication configuration screen.

14. Within the Azure portal **App registration** window, go to **Authentication** on the left navigation. You will be presented with a screen like the following screenshot:

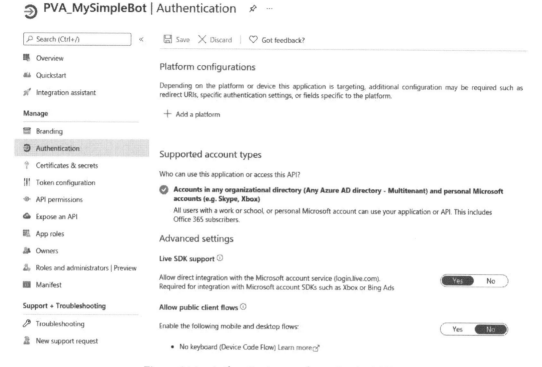

Figure 6.14 – Authentication configuration in AAD

15. If you have not completed **Redirect URI** in *Step 9* above, select the **Add a platform** button, and in the new area displayed, select the **Web** option.

16. When asked to provide a redirect URL, put in the following address: `https://token.botframework.com/.auth/web/redirect`.

17. Select both options for **Access tokens** and **ID tokens**, as shown in the following screenshot:

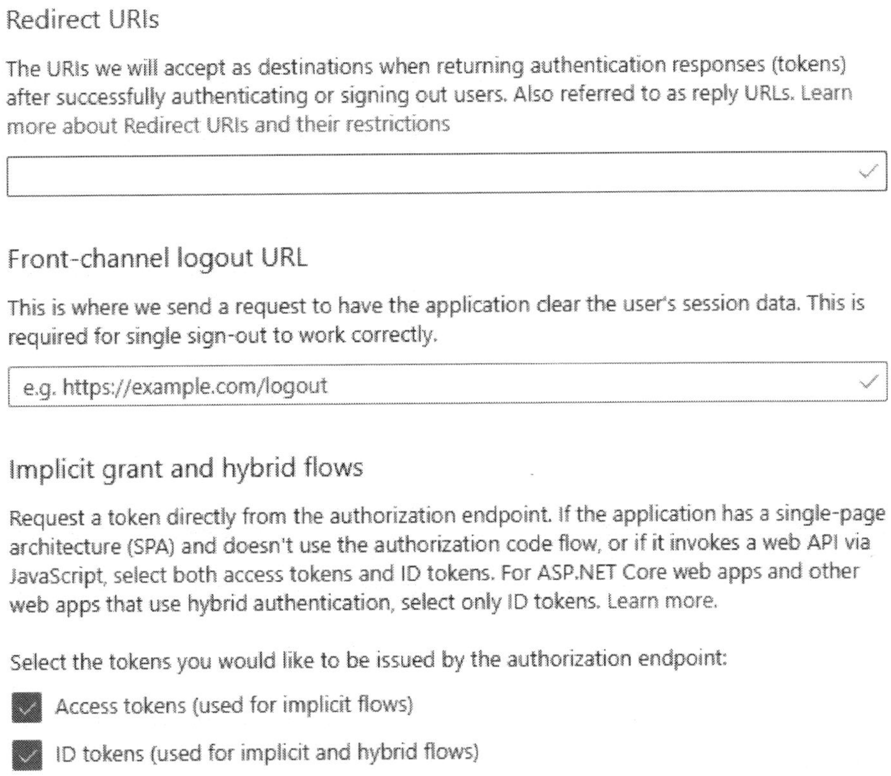

Redirect URIs

The URIs we will accept as destinations when returning authentication responses (tokens) after successfully authenticating or signing out users. Also referred to as reply URLs. Learn more about Redirect URIs and their restrictions

Front-channel logout URL

This is where we send a request to have the application clear the user's session data. This is required for single sign-out to work correctly.

> e.g. https://example.com/logout

Implicit grant and hybrid flows

Request a token directly from the authorization endpoint. If the application has a single-page architecture (SPA) and doesn't use the authorization code flow, or if it invokes a web API via JavaScript, select both access tokens and ID tokens. For ASP.NET Core web apps and other web apps that use hybrid authentication, select only ID tokens. Learn more.

Select the tokens you would like to be issued by the authorization endpoint:

☑ Access tokens (used for implicit flows)

☑ ID tokens (used for implicit and hybrid flows)

Figure 6.15 – Configure web section

18. When done, click on the **Configure** button.

19. Next, in the Azure portal, with an admin account, select the **API permissions** area in the left menu. Here, select **Grant admin consent**, and on the popup, select **Yes**, as shown in the following screenshot.

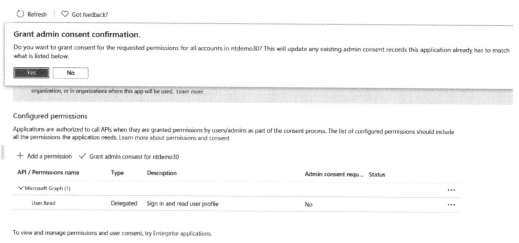

Figure 6.16 – Grant consent for the organization

20. Next, we need to define a scope for our virtual agent. In the Azure admin portal, select on the left navigation the **Expose an API** option. On the page presented, select **Add a scope**, and populate **Application ID URI**. This is a unique URI used to identify this application, and you can use the default provided by the platform, as shown in the following screenshot:

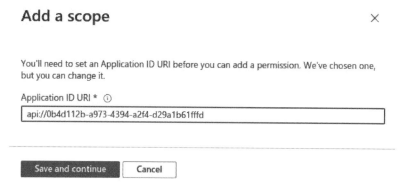

Figure 6.17 – Expose an API

21. On the next screen, configure the scope by providing a name and providing details in the other fields. The following screenshot shows a possible configuration:

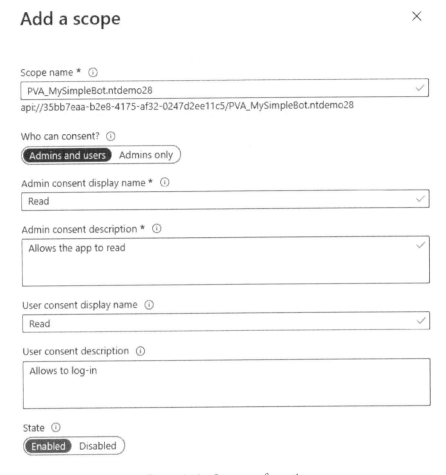

Figure 6.18 – Scope configuration

22. When done, select the **Add scope** button. This returns you to the **Expose an API** page and provides you with the Scope URI, which is what you need to populate in the **Token exchange URL** field on the agent authentication configuration page.

23. Finally, we need a client secret to complete the configuration for our chatbot authentication. In the Azure admin portal, navigate on the left side to **Certificates & secrets**, and select on the page the **New client** secret. In the newly generated record, copy the **Value** field and populate it into the virtual agent authentication configuration page's **Client secret** field. Note that these are confidential information and should be secured as such.

24. Select **Save** when complete. You are prompted to confirm and are notified that you need to re-publish the bot for the authentication settings to take effect. Click **Save** again, then select **Close**.

25. Now, let's change the default greeting topic to ask for authentication. We can simply change the last message to say `Can you tell me who you are?`, then add an **Authenticate** action. This will look like the following screenshot:

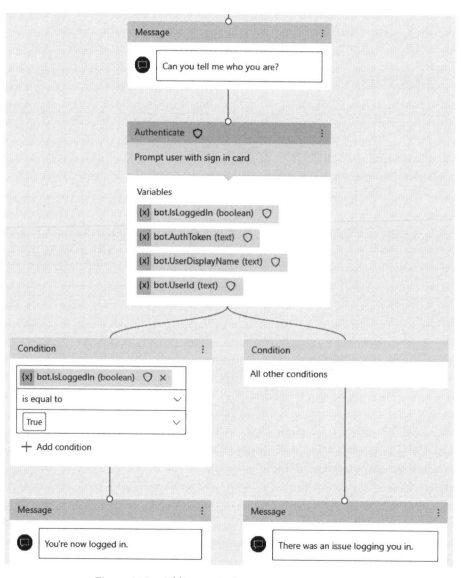

Figure 6.19 – Adding an Authenticate action to a topic

26. On the agent page, select **Publish** and re-publish the bot. Now you should be able to test the login functionality on the demo website for your virtual agent.

27. Navigate to the Power Virtual Agents demo website for your bot, start with a greeting, and, when prompted, select the **Login** option. A new window will prompt you to authenticate and will provide a numeric code for validation. Enter this code into the chat window, and you should get the **You're now logged in** message, as shown in the following screenshot:

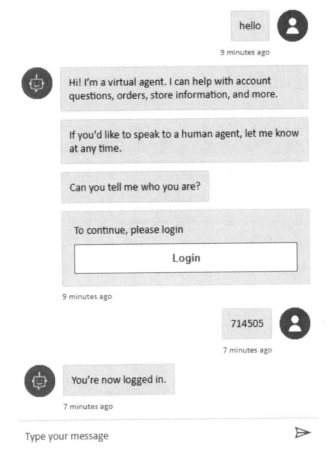

Figure 6.20 – Login successful

This was a slightly more complex scenario that we covered. We required a little bit of setup on the Azure side to register our application so we could provide the proper authentication to our virtual agent.

Let's next look at some considerations for authentication.

Authentication considerations

Now that we have seen how to configure authentication in our virtual agent, let's look at a couple of common scenarios as to why you might want to do that.

First off, knowing who you are interacting with opens the door for new possibilities. You can start providing a personalized experience. Some of the things you can do include the following:

- Create a personalized look and feel for the entire user experience.
- Personalize conversations, with data included from various data sources and specific to that particular customer.
- Accept files uploaded by a specific user against their current account.
- Provide specific data from backend systems, relevant to the user logged in.
- Pass to a live agent the correct details for the already authenticated user.

Again, these are just some common scenarios.

In addition, we have only looked at the ability to authenticate against Azure Active Directory. The platform also allows us to authenticate against any **OAuth 2** identity provider. What does that mean for us? We can simply integrate this functionality into other non-Microsoft environments. This makes the platform flexible and applicable to almost any environment using this authentication standard. It also allows us to pass the authenticated credentials into backend systems using this same authentication mechanism, whether online SaaS solutions or on-premises.

You can now see how this is an unbelievably valuable capability.

Let's next have a quick look at how we can use this authentication to provide even more value to the user.

Leveraging various data sources

In recent years, it has become common for organizations that serve many customers to provide a self-service portal. This functionality allows a user to log in to their profile and perform various actions, such as retrieving and paying monthly bills, opening support tickets, updating personal information, and so on.

Providing a virtual agent to assist with some of these tasks can sometimes simplify the user experience, thus enhancing customer satisfaction.

Imagine the following scenario, where I have to log in to my profile on a self-service portal and retrieve information about my last bill. I would have to log in to that portal, find the billing area, find the last bill, open it, and see the outstanding balance.

What if I could simply interact with a virtual agent, log in, and simply ask the question: What is my outstanding balance? The bot would simply retrieve that from a backend **Customer Relationship Management** (**CRM**) system, and provide that to me directly, possibly with a link to process the payment.

Isn't that a much simpler user experience?

This can be achieved by using Power Virtual Agents, along with authentication. And this is only one simple scenario – there are many more.

Summary

Congratulations, you have completed the main topics on Power Virtual Agents.

In this chapter, we looked at expanding our bot's capabilities by providing content indexed from various sources, such as public FAQ pages. We also looked at authenticating users to provide personalized services.

With these additional capabilities, we can now start building relatively complex agents that provide an experience much closer to a real human agent. By understating who the customer is, and providing a wide range of information, both personalized as well as generic products, services, or company details, we can shape scenarios that will provide all the necessary information to our users, without the need to involve our existing support staff. And this is the main purpose of these Power Virtual Agents. We want to offload the mundane and repetitive tasks to automation, to leave enough time for our support agents to focus on resolving complex problems for our customers.

The second half of this book takes us further by discussing how Power Virtual Agents applies to the Teams collaboration environment. We will be shifting our attention from servicing external users, such as customers and partners, to internal users, our staff. The next chapter introduces the Power Virtual Agents for Teams environment and the process of creating an agent for Teams.

Section 3: Leveraging Power Virtual Agents in Teams

This section handles scenarios where we serve conversational support to internal stakeholders and team members. The Power Virtual Agents scenarios presented will be surfaced through Microsoft Teams to internal users.

This section contains the following chapters:

- *Chapter 7, Building a Power Virtual Agents Application for Teams*
- *Chapter 8, Integrating the Power Virtual Agent into Teams*
- *Chapter 9, Serving Information from Various Sources*

7

Building a Power Virtual Agents Application for Teams

In the first half of this book, we focused our attention on **Power Virtual Agents** servicing a large audience by exposing them through a public website. Their role was to handle requests from people outside our organization.

From now on, we will shift our attention to servicing users within our organization. We will look at bots exposed to our team members through the familiar **Microsoft Teams** interface.

In this chapter, we will tackle the following topics:

- Description of the business scenario
- Creating a Power Virtual Agents application for Teams

As part of the presented scenario, we will be revisiting topics such as decision logic and guiding the conversation.

At the end of this chapter, we will have our first Power Virtual Agents application for Teams. We will see how to make decisions based on the user request and profile, and, as we have seen with Power Virtual Agents for the web, we will guide the conversation with predetermined options to select from.

So, let's get going!

Description of the business scenario

For the purpose of this introductory chapter to Power Virtual Agents for Teams, we will look at creating a simple **human resources (HR)** chatbot for Teams that will return information about holidays and remaining vacation days. A user will be able to interact with the chatbot and request details on holidays for the current year, as well as to get more personalized information about their respective remaining vacation days.

As you will see, the process to create a chatbot is, for Teams, quite similar to the one for creating a chatbot for the web. The **user interface (UI)** is identical, and the topics and actions are created in a similar fashion. The main difference stems from the fact that, while exposing the chatbot through Teams, we now have context about the user interacting with the chatbot, and we have no need to process the user authentication.

Let's see next how to build our first Power Virtual Agents application for Teams.

Creating a Power Virtual Agents application for Teams

When creating chatbots for Teams, we work directly within Teams.

Teams has gained a lot of popularity and is becoming the standard platform for enterprise collaboration. It offers abilities beyond the standard chat functionality and voice or video conferencing. It acts as a central collaboration hub, having tight integration with the Office suite of applications, as well as a variety of additional services. Besides the most obvious services—such as file storage and sharing, along with versioning control powered by SharePoint—it also allows various external applications to be brought in.

For us to build our first chatbot, we need to add the Power Virtual Agents application to Teams. This is done by going along the left navigation bar to the ellipsis and retrieving the Power Virtual Agents application, as seen in the following screenshot:

Figure 7.1 – Adding Power Virtual Agents to Teams

If Power Virtual Agents does not show up directly in the **Recent** section, use the search bar at the top to find it, as presented in the previous screenshot.

Once you select the **Power Virtual Agents** option, you are presented with a screen overlay describing the application, as well as an **Add** option to add it to your version of Teams, as shown in the following screenshot:

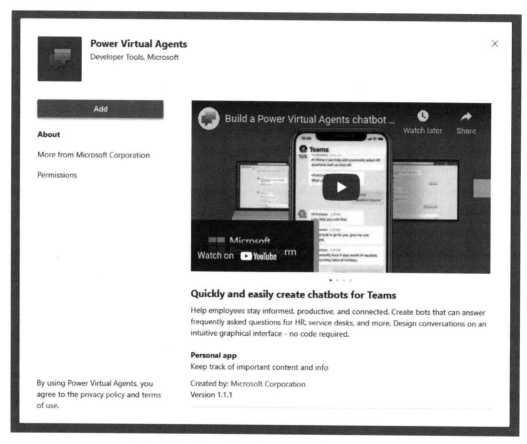

Figure 7.2 – Power Virtual Agents application overlay

Select the **Add** button, and **Power Virtual Agents** will be shown on the side navigation ribbon, as seen in the following screenshot:

Figure 7.3 – Power Virtual Agents application on the Teams navigation ribbon

In order to make sure that the application always remains visible, you can simply right-click on the icon and from the pop-up menu select the **Pin** option, as shown in the following screenshot:

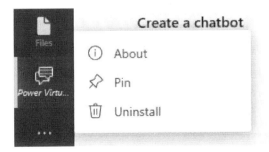

Figure 7.4 – Pinning the Power Virtual Agents application

Your Power Virtual Agents application will now always be available and visible on the navigation ribbon. You can navigate to any of the other applications, and then return easily to it.

Now that we have the housekeeping out of the way, let's build our first chatbot.

Right at the top of the **Power Virtual Agents** window, we are presented with a simple navigation bar, as seen in the following screenshot:

Power Virtual Agents
Home
Chatbots
About
Empower employees, one chat at a time
Give people access to the help they need, 24/7. Automate frequently asked questions and common business processes for HR, service desks, and more.

Figure 7.5 – Power Virtual Agents navigation bar

The **Home** tab presents generic information about the application, documentation about creating chatbots, and an option to create a new chatbot.

The **Chatbots** tab presents a list of chatbots already created. If none have been created, you will only see an option to create a new chatbot.

Finally, the **About** tab presents the application version and description, along with links to the Power Virtual Agents website, the **Privacy policy**, and the **Terms of use**.

Let's go to the **Chatbots** tab and select the **New chatbot** button to generate our new chatbot. This opens up an overlay window where you are prompted to select a specific team as the target of your new chatbot, as seen in the following screenshot:

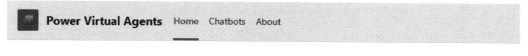

Figure 7.6 – Creating a chatbot

Since this is the first chatbot created for the **All Employees** team, you are notified that some background setup will take place. If you don't already have a team created, you should create one before this step.

Click on **Continue** and wait for the system to complete all background processes. The following screenshot shows the window you will see at this stage:

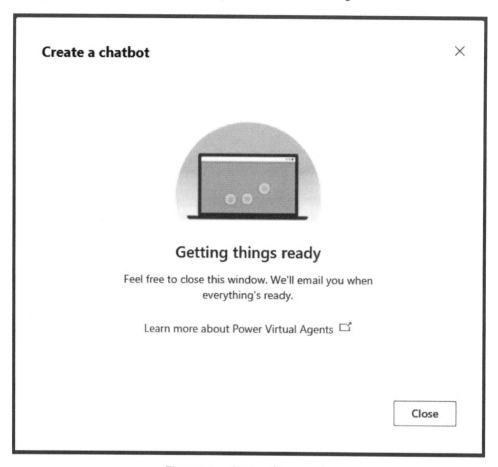

Figure 7.7 – Getting things ready

You can click **Close** to close this window while the process continues. You will be notified when it completes.

Once it is all done, the screen will refresh, showing the **All Employees** team and an option to create chatbots for it, as shown in the following screenshot:

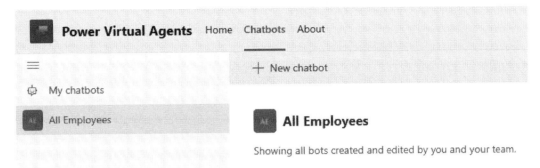

Figure 7.8 – Team chatbots

Select the **All Employees** team and then select the **+ New chatbot** option to generate the first chatbot for this team. This brings up the bot creation wizard, as seen in the following screenshot:

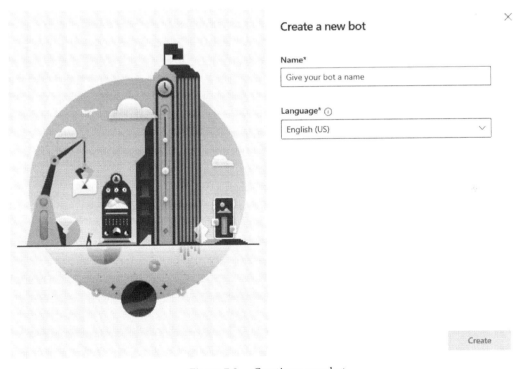

Figure 7.9 – Creating a new bot

Give your bot a name. Let's call ours **Time off inquiry**. Click on **Create** when done. A **Creating your bot** window displays while the bot is created, after which the screen refreshes, and you are presented with the already familiar interface to create new chatbots. This is similar to the interface we have already used when creating Power Virtual Agents for the web, as seen in the following screenshot:

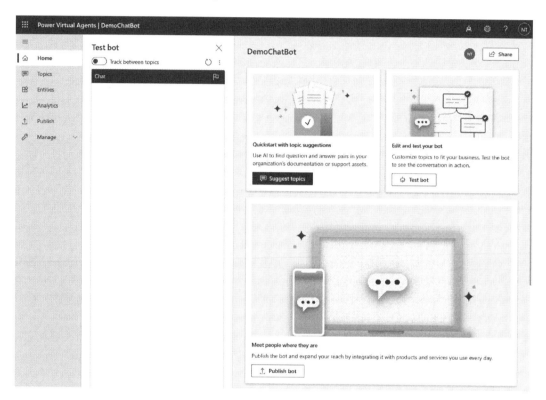

Figure 7.10 – Bot editor window

Navigating to **Topics**, we will find the same topics we have already seen when creating chatbots for the web. We can test this bot functionality using the **Test bot** window, and we can create new topics as needed.

Let's create a **Time off inquiry** topic in the following steps:

1. Select from the top options the **New topic** button.

2. Give it a name of **Time off inquiry** and add a few trigger phrases, as seen in the following screenshot:

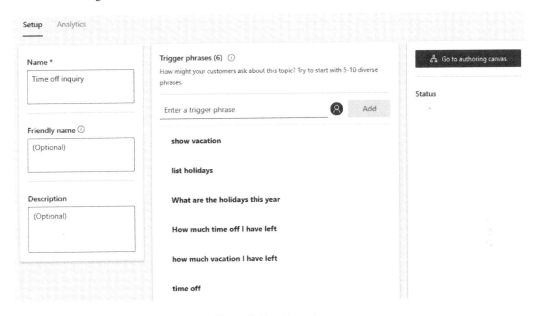

Figure 7.11 – Bot setup

3. Next, click the **Go to authoring canvas** button to create the chatbot behavior.

4. By default, the authoring canvas shows the trigger phrases and a **Message** block following that. Let's remove this **Message** block, and instead add an **Ask a question** action.

5. As we remember from creating a chatbot for the web, each possible response is placed on its own branch of logic, as seen in the following screenshot:

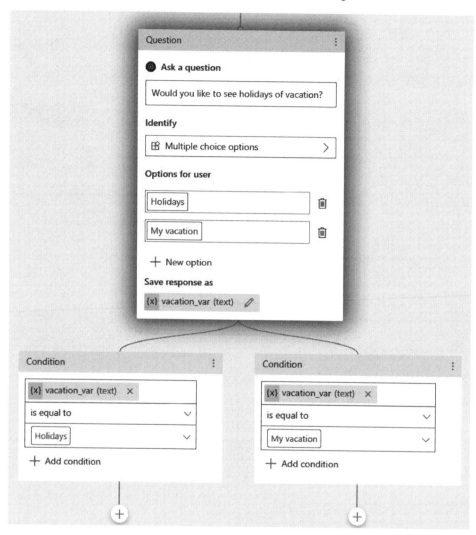

Figure 7.12 – Question branching

6. Let's first handle the **Holidays** branch, as this will only return a fixed message. We can add a **Message** block after the condition and populate the message with text describing the available holidays this year, as seen in the following screenshot:

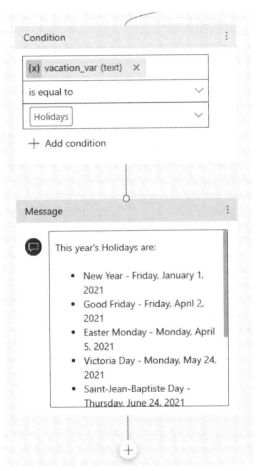

Figure 7.13 – Holidays message

7. For the **My vacation** branch, instead of showing a simple message, we will retrieve some details dynamically using a Power Automate flow. Let's use the **Call an action** option, as seen in the following screenshot:

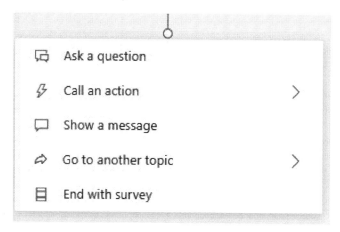

Figure 7.14 – Call an action option

8. From the window that opens, find and select the existing flow that returns the remaining vacation days' value. Note that in my case, this flow is already built into the system.

> **Important note**
> Power Automate flow creation is a complex topic outside the scope of this title. We will touch on the basics of Power Automate in *Chapter 9, Serving Information from Various Sources*, but for a fully comprehensive understanding, you should refer to the Microsoft documentation, available at `https://docs.microsoft.com/en-us/power-automate/`.

The following screenshot shows the flow selection window:

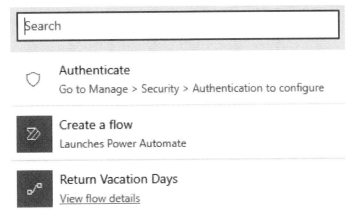

Figure 7.15 – Return Vacation Days flow

9. Your action added to the Power Virtual Agent editing canvas will look like this:

Figure 7.16 – Calling Power Automate flow action

10. Finally, we can add a **Message** block that shows the user the number of vacation days available. We display the name of the user in the message by selecting the default `bot.UserDisplayName` variable, along with the value of the `VacationDays` (number) variable that was populated by the Power Automate flow. Other variables presented here include the default `bot.UserId` variable that returns the internal ID for the current user, as well the custom `vacation_var` temporary variable we created. Selecting the output of the flow is done on the message by clicking the variable dropdown in the **Message** menu and selecting the variable name, as shown in the following screenshot:

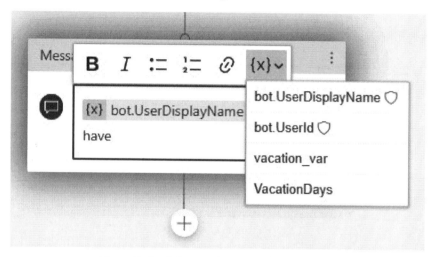

Figure 7.17 – Selecting the output from the flow

11. Your complete branch for **My vacation** will look like this:

Figure 7.18 – Complete My vacation branch

Now, let's test the chatbot functionality. We can use the **Test bot** section and interact with our chatbot. We first ask it for **time off**, and in the choices, we select **Holidays**. The output will look like this:

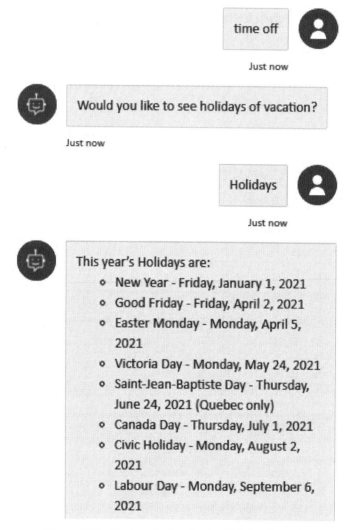

Figure 7.19 – Testing chatbot for the Holidays branch

Alternatively, we can test the **My vacation** branch, with the output presented in the following screenshot:

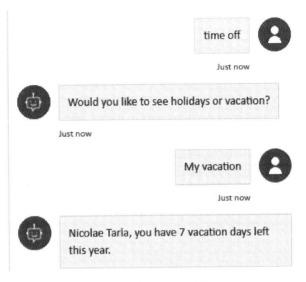

Figure 7.20 – Testing chatbot for the My vacation branch

Note that, based on the trigger phrases we created and the way the chatbot is built, you could ask a direct question and the bot will get you past all the chit-chat and straight to the answer. We can see this represented in the following screenshot:

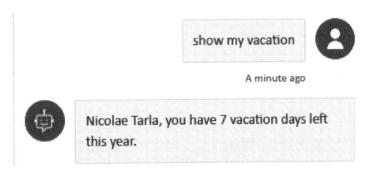

Figure 7.21 – Bypassing the chit-chat

Congratulations— you now have your first Power Virtual Agents application for Teams!

Summary

In this chapter, we looked at a simplified business scenario, leveraging a Power Virtual Agents application for Teams. We created an agent, expanded on its functionality by adding some business logic, and provided some guidance to the user in the form's predetermined answers to select from.

While the similarities with chatbots for the web are obvious, we now have an understanding of how to create a chatbot for Teams. We have an understanding of the fact that a user in Teams is automatically recognized, and we can provide a much more personalized experience enhanced by information from other integrated systems and platforms.

The presented example is a highly simplified one, but imagine the possibilities of creating such a chatbot to fully manage your vacation request cycle. You could first ask for a listing of standard holidays to determine whether your planned vacation overlaps with any of those days and then determine the remaining vacation days for the current year, followed by directly submitting a new vacation request based on the previous information. You could even encounter some validation in the process, whereby if a user requests more vacation than is available, the request is automatically rejected, with a message informing the user of what the issue is. This entire process would then send an email to the user's manager for approval. The manager would approve it directly from the email, and the platform would track all these details, with minimal user interaction. This is a good research topic to continue and expand your knowledge.

In the next chapter, we will look at how this chatbot is exposed and will also explore functions within Microsoft Teams.

8
Integrating the Power Virtual Agent into Teams

In the previous chapter, we built our first chatbot for Teams. The overall creation experience is similar to creating chatbots for the web, but the target audience is entirely different.

This chapter focuses on taking a Power Virtual Agent chatbot created for Teams and presenting it to a Teams audience. We will be looking at various ways of making a chatbot available to Teams members.

In this chapter, we will tackle the following topics:

- Where can we introduce a Power Virtual Agent for Teams?
- How to present our Power Virtual Agent for Teams
- One Power Virtual Agent versus many

At the end of this chapter, we will have our first Power Virtual Agent for Teams presented to the internal users of our organization. We will understand where and how we can present this chatbot while revisiting the topic of a single chatbot versus multiple chatbots servicing a set of requests.

So, let's get going!

Where can we introduce a Power Virtual Agent for Teams?

In *Chapter 7, Building a Power Virtual Agents Application for Teams*, we created our first **Time off inquiry** bot to respond to users' questions about holidays and their respective remaining time off. Once done with the creation of the bot, we published it to make it available to the organization. On the publishing screen, once publishing is complete, you are presented with an option to **Open the bot**, as seen in the following screenshot:

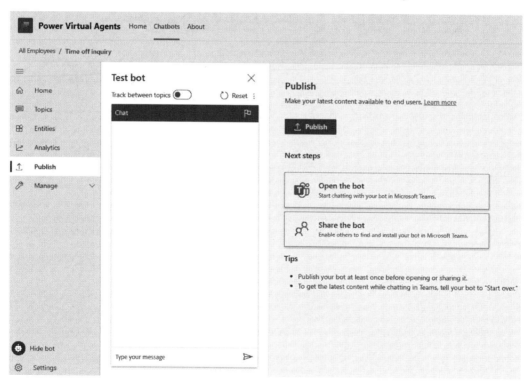

Figure 8.1 – Bot publishing screen

You can select the **Open to bot** button and start interacting with our agent directly on Teams.

Selecting this option prompts you to install the agent, as depicted in *Figure 8.2*:

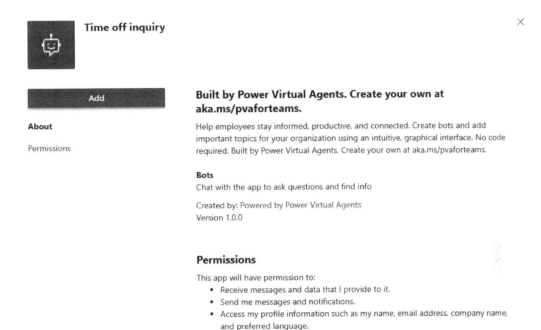

Figure 8.2 – Adding the Time off inquiry bot

You can review the permissions, and then select the **Add** button. Once added, it will be presented on the left navigation on Teams, as shown in *Figure 8.3*:

Figure 8.3 – Time off inquiry bot on Teams navigation

Selecting this option presents you with the window to start interacting with your chatbot. Following a short conversation, your output could resemble the following screenshot:

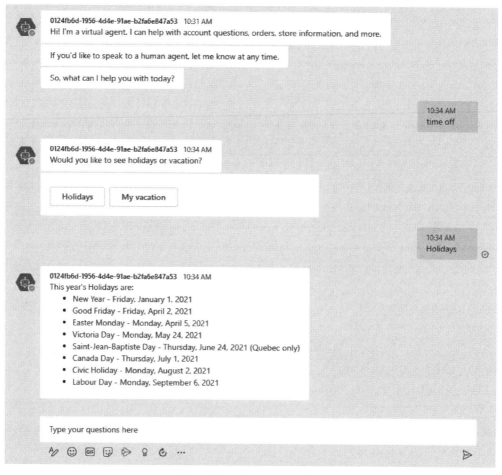

Figure 8.4 – Bot conversation

Just like we can pin any other apps, we can also select this chatbot and pin it to the navigation so it's always available to easily go back to. You do this by right-clicking on the navigation item and selecting the **Pin** option from the pop-up menu, as shown in *Figure 8.5*:

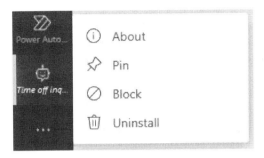

Figure 8.5 – Pinning the bot to the navigation

Now that our bot is published, let's look in the next section at some ways to make it available to the organization.

How to present our Power Virtual Agent for Teams

With a bot published, we have several options to present it to our users. These include the following:

1. With the bot installed in Teams, we can share a link to it with other users.

2. We can share the bot with the team by adding it to the **Built by your colleagues'** section in the Microsoft Teams app store.

3. We can share the bot with the entire organization by submitting it for admin approval. This will place it in the **Published by your org** area of the Microsoft Teams app store.

4. We can distribute it within the tenant using the pre-generated app manifest.

The first and second options primarily handle bots created by power users and that are meant to be shared with a subset of users of your organization. This is along the lines of personal productivity.

Options three and four target the entire organization. Since option number four is the most advanced and allows for making detailed changes to the manifest document directly before sharing, we will regard that as a more developer-focused option. We will focus our attention instead on option number three.

Sharing a bot with your organization by submitting it for admin approval

Microsoft Teams allows various applications to be installed. Depending on the security restrictions applied to your organization, you could install organization-specific apps or external apps. Some of these are provided by Microsoft, while others are third-party applications created specifically to integrate other services into your Teams organization.

You can see a list of available applications by navigating in Teams to the apps on the navigation, as presented in the following screenshot:

Figure 8.6 – Installing additional apps in Teams

Once you select this option, you are presented with a list of categories and applications that are available to be installed, as presented in *Figure 8.7*:

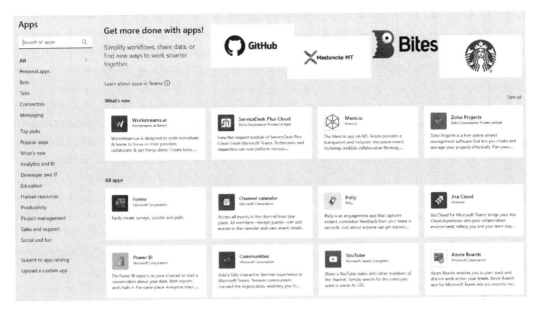

Figure 8.7 – Apps available for Teams

As you can see, a large number of apps are available. If we now search for our Time off inquiry chatbot, nothing is returned, as shown in *Figure 8.8*:

Figure 8.8 – No results returned

The reason for this is because, while our chatbot is published, it is not shared with the organization.

Let's now see how we can publish this chatbot to the organization by submitting it for admin approval:

1. In Teams, navigate to **Power Virtual Agents** and find the chatbot, as shown in the following screenshot:

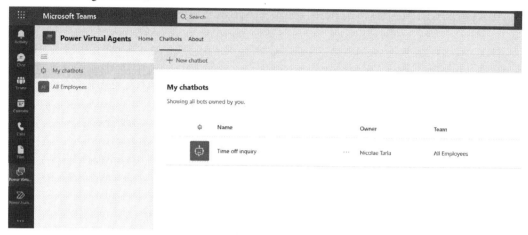

Figure 8.9 – Finding the chatbot to be published

2. Open the chatbot for editing by selecting the ellipsis and choosing the **Edit** option in the menu provided.

3. Select the **Publish** option and then choose the **Share the bot** button, as shown in the following screenshot:

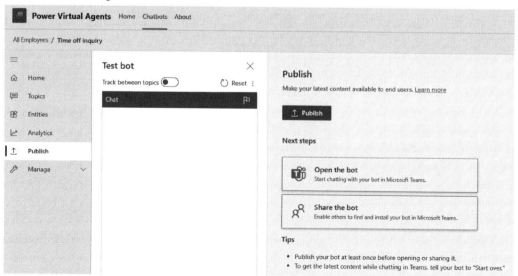

Figure 8.10 – Share the bot

4. A new overlay opens on the right side of the screen, as shown in the following screenshot:

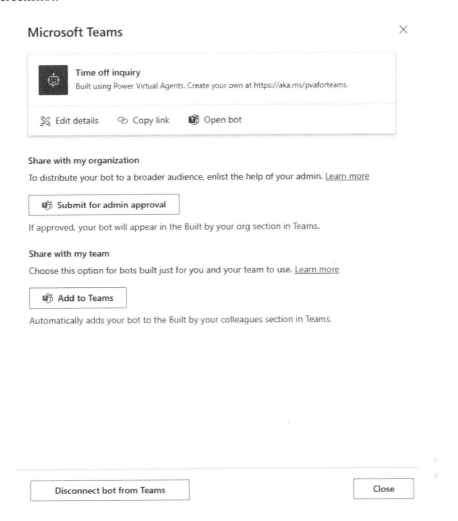

Figure 8.11 – Teams publishing

5. Select the **Submit for admin approval** option presented. This opens the next wizard screen, as shown in the following screenshot:

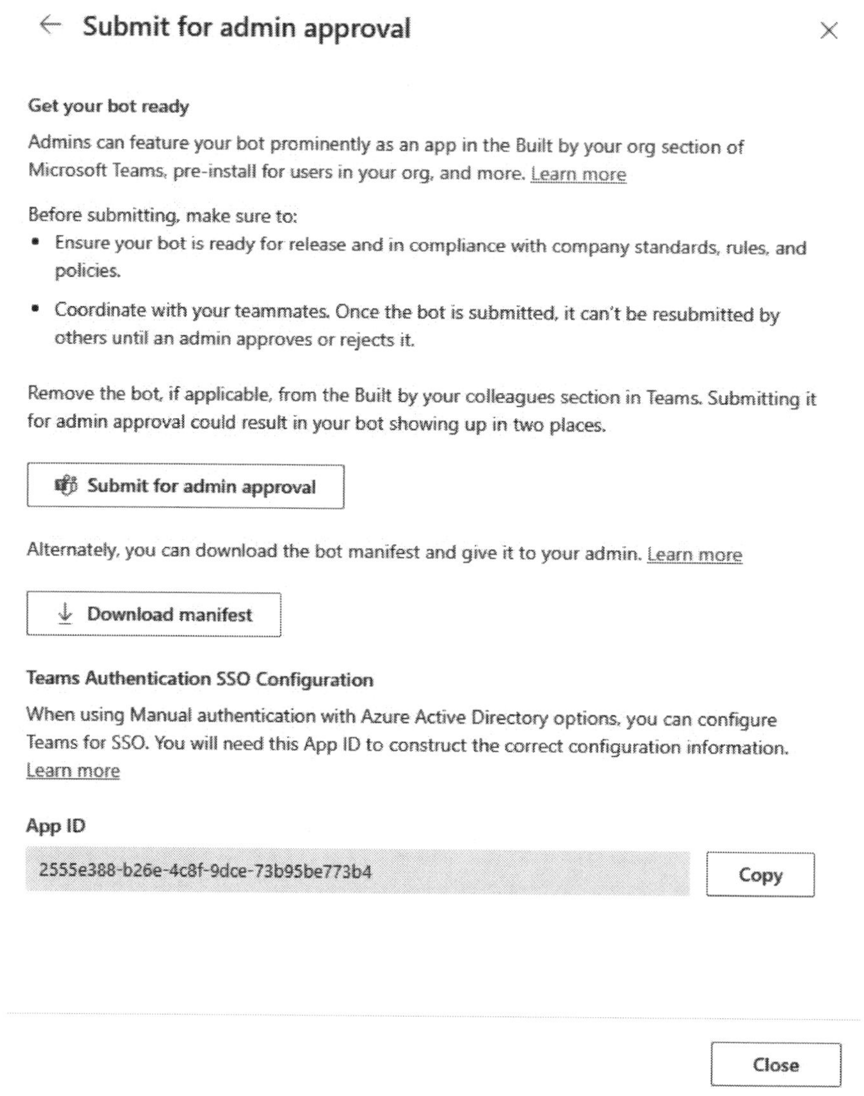

← **Submit for admin approval**   ✕

Get your bot ready

Admins can feature your bot prominently as an app in the Built by your org section of Microsoft Teams, pre-install for users in your org, and more. Learn more

Before submitting, make sure to:

*   Ensure your bot is ready for release and in compliance with company standards, rules, and policies.

*   Coordinate with your teammates. Once the bot is submitted, it can't be resubmitted by others until an admin approves or rejects it.

Remove the bot, if applicable, from the Built by your colleagues section in Teams. Submitting it for admin approval could result in your bot showing up in two places.

[🖽 Submit for admin approval]

Alternately, you can download the bot manifest and give it to your admin. Learn more

[↓ Download manifest]

Teams Authentication SSO Configuration

When using Manual authentication with Azure Active Directory options, you can configure Teams for SSO. You will need this App ID to construct the correct configuration information. Learn more

App ID

| 2555e388-b26e-4c8f-9dce-73b95be773b4 | | Copy |

[Close]

Figure 8.12 – Submit for admin approval

6. Select the **Submit for admin approval** option on this screen. This takes you to a new screen where you configure the icon presented in Teams, as well as the short and long description, as seen in the following screenshot:

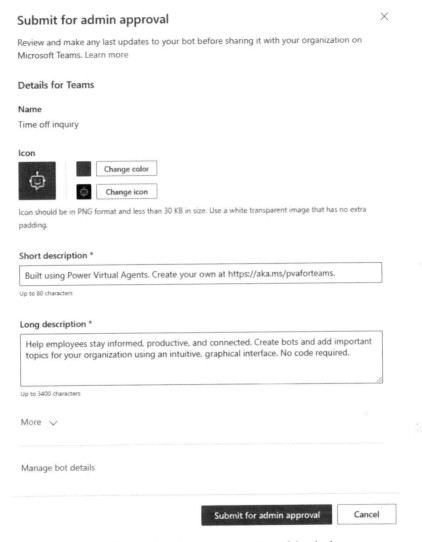

Figure 8.13 – Configuring the presentation of the chatbot

7. Expanding the **More** option allows you to configure items such as the developer's name, where you might want to specify the group that created and supports this chatbot, along with Microsoft Partner Network ID, and track whether an external partner provides support.

8. Finally, when ready, select the **Submit for admin approval** button. You are prompted to confirm that everyone within the organization will have access to this chatbot, as shown in the following screenshot:

Figure 8.14 – Final confirmation

9. Select **Yes** on this screen. The bot is not submitted to admins for approval, and you should see a confirmation screen, as shown in the following screenshot:

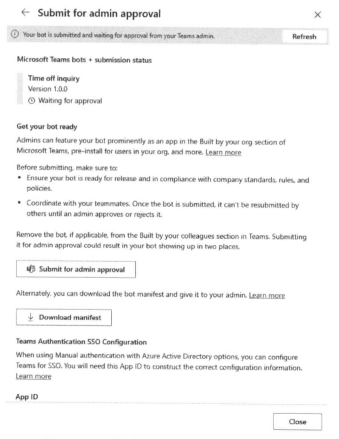

Figure 8.15 – Chatbot submission confirmation

10. Select **Close** to complete the submission process.

Now your chatbot is waiting for admin approval before it can be presented to all users. The approval process is done through the Teams admin console and is outside the scope of this title. This is a Teams administration-specific function. If you are simply following through these steps in a trial environment and want to perform those steps, please refer to the Teams administration documentation available at the following URL:

```
https://docs.microsoft.com/en-us/microsoftteams/submit-
approve-custom-apps
```

Once you have the application approved by an administrator, it will show up when you search for it by going to the ellipsis on the navigation and searching the name in the search box, as seen in the following screenshot:

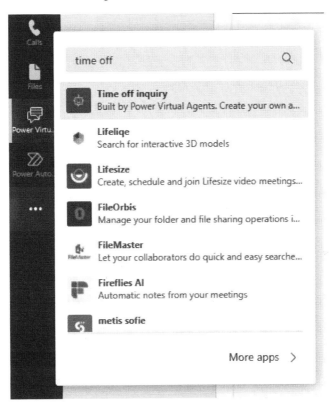

Figure 8.16 – Finding an app

It will also show up in the Apps listing for your organization.

Let's have a look next at the value of having separate chatbots versus cramming all functionality into a single bot.

One Power Virtual Agent versus many

As we mentioned in *Chapter 5, Integrating a Power Virtual Agent into Your Website*, we want to take an incremental approach to creating chatbots for Teams. You want to gauge the success, make improvements, and expand on that functionality as needed.

Just as we use Topics to segment different discussion paths within a chatbot definition, we can take a similar approach to define our individual chatbots. We do not want to bring to our user a single HR chatbot, for example, with all HR supporting functionalities baked into it. This will make it more difficult to maintain in the future.

In such scenarios, we want to consider the possibility of creating multiple chatbots for specific functionality. For example, in the context of functionality provided by the HR department in your organization, you could have one or more of the following chatbots:

- HR Time Off chatbot – Handling queries around holidays, available vacation, and future vacation requests

- HR Compensation chatbot – Handling requests related to compensation

- HR Benefits Support chatbot – Handling requests regarding benefits, benefit forms, and suchlike

Since these are distinct requests and could be receiving updates at different time intervals, which could be handled with input from different members of the HR department, it only makes sense to have them separated into different chatbots that can be maintained individually. In addition, by taking this approach, you can monitor performance and usage and determine where the most effort in updates should be focused. This also helps mitigate any possible session limitations imposed by the platform.

Summary

In this chapter, we looked at surfacing a Power Virtual Agent into Teams and making it available to our Teams users across the organization. We then looked at where it makes sense to create multiple chatbots serving different functions.

After reviewing this chapter, we should have a good understanding of the various ways in which we can make a chatbot available in Teams, from a simple process of sharing a chatbot to full-blown publishing and approval by the Teams administrator.

In the next chapter, we will focus on the details around bringing information from external data sources into our Power Virtual Agents and serving that information to users through chat.

9
Serving Information from Various Sources

In the previous chapter, we looked at presenting our chatbot in Teams. The user experience is now targeted specifically at authenticated users. We now can determine the type of information we return based on the user's permissions and access to that information.

This chapter focuses on providing contextual information back to users. Knowing who the user interacting with our chatbot is, we can easily determine the type of information returned, based on that respective user's permissions and access to the information.

In this chapter, we will tackle the following topics:

- The role of connectors in a Power Virtual Agents conversation
- Retrieving data using available connectors
- Retrieving data from other sources

At the end of this chapter, we will have a comprehensive understanding of how Power Virtual Agents interacts with external systems to retrieve relevant data and use that data in our chat conversation. This is extremely important, as it makes out chatbots much more relevant to our users.

So, let's look at the connectors first to understand how we can achieve these integrations!

The role of connectors in a Power Virtual Agents conversation

In *Chapter 8, Integrating the Power Virtual Agent into Teams*, we used an example where we questioned an HR chatbot about our remaining vacation time, and it was able to respond with the exact number of vacation days remaining for the user. We mentioned in passing that we used a Power Automate flow to achieve this.

An important aspect to understand is that Power Automate, just like most of the Power Platform, leverages a large set of connectors to tap into other external applications and perform various **Create**, **Read**, **Update** or **Delete** (**CRUD**) operations. The most common one with chatbots is, as expected, **Read**. We want our chatbot to return relevant information to the user it converses with, and to do that, the chatbot needs to read that information from various sources.

But let's make a distinction between static and dynamic data before we delve into how data is retrieved and introduced into a conversation.

Static data is your typical information that does not change much over time. It might not change at all, or might be reviewed on a schedule, maybe annually. I am referring primarily to data such as a set of support how-to documents or help pages. Once created, this data remains pretty static and might be reviewed at time intervals based on user feedback. This does not happen daily, or even weekly or quarterly, in most circumstances. Hence, we look at this as static data, and we can take a more simplistic approach to surfacing these sets of information. We can simply index and let the chatbot platform generate topics based on this data. Next time this data is refreshed, we can simply follow the same process to re-generate our topics.

Dynamic data, on the other hand, is data that is actively used in other applications and can receive updates at random intervals, sometimes several times a day. Think of your typical sales application, where you track all contact points with a client, requests for documentation, leads and opportunities, updates to account and contact details, and many more. This type of data can potentially change often. This is a request to show all active opportunities at the time the request is made. Hopefully, the results presented in the afternoon will be slightly different from the results from that morning, meaning your sales team is actually working on the opportunities, adding new ones, and possibly closing some existing ones. This is where the approach is different from working with static data. We cannot simply index this and present it to users; we need to retrieve this information in real time or near-real time to capture the most up-to-date status. We use, in this situation, a Power Automate flow and connectors to retrieve our data on demand.

Let's start by revisiting the static data presentation method by creating a set of topics from a static public page presenting documentation.

Working with static data

To create topics based on an existing help page, we achieve this by following these steps:

1. In the chatbot editor, select the **Topics** option, as shown in the following screenshot:

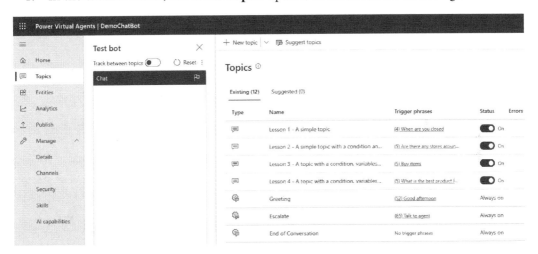

Figure 9.1 – Topics on the chatbot editor

2. On the top ribbon, find and select the **Suggest topics** button. This will present a wizard window, as shown in the following screenshot:

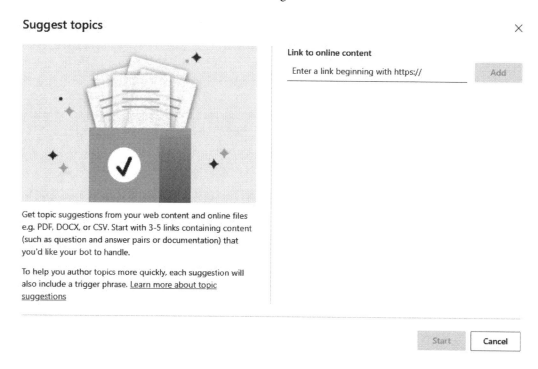

Figure 9.2 – Topic wizard window

3. An important aspect of this approach is the ability to generate topic material from one or more sources at a time. In addition, you are not limited to simple web pages, but you can easily point the process to documents such as PDFs, Word documents, or **Comma-Separated Values (CSV)** files. This allows us to capture multiple documentation materials related to a product, for example, and include them all together in the generated topics. For simplicity, let's point our process to one of the Microsoft documentation pages on Docs. I will be using the following page, but you can select any other page you like: `https://docs.microsoft.com/en-us/power-virtual-agents/authoring-create-edit-topics`.

4. Once you populate one or more target destinations for topics to create from, the **Start** button is activated. Click on **Start**.

5. A notification message pops up showing the system is processing the information, as shown in the following screenshot:

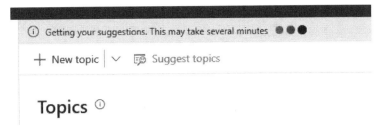

Figure 9.3 – Processing topic values

6. Once the processing is complete, you will get a notification with the number of topics generated. Select the **Suggested** tab and you will see all topics generated. The following screenshot shows this:

You have 13 new topic suggestions.

+ New topic | ∨ | Suggest topics

Topics ⓘ

Existing (12)   **Suggested (13)**

Name	Trigger phrases	Source	Received
Create and edit topics in your Power Virtual Ag...	Create and edit topics in your Powe...	https://docs.microsoft.com/en-us/p...	5/5/2021, 10:29 AM
Use system and sample topics	Use system and sample topics	https://docs.microsoft.com/en-us/p...	5/5/2021, 10:29 AM
Create a topic	Create a topic	https://docs.microsoft.com/en-us/p...	5/5/2021, 10:29 AM
Design the topic's conversation path	Design the topic's conversation path	https://docs.microsoft.com/en-us/p...	5/5/2021, 10:29 AM
Insert nodes - Design the topic's conversation ...	Insert nodes - Design the topic's co...	https://docs.microsoft.com/en-us/p...	5/5/2021, 10:29 AM
Ask a question:	Ask a question:	https://docs.microsoft.com/en-us/p...	5/5/2021, 10:29 AM
Call an action	Call an action	https://docs.microsoft.com/en-us/p...	5/5/2021, 10:29 AM
Show a message	Show a message	https://docs.microsoft.com/en-us/p...	5/5/2021, 10:29 AM
Go to another topic	Go to another topic	https://docs.microsoft.com/en-us/p...	5/5/2021, 10:29 AM
End the conversation	End the conversation	https://docs.microsoft.com/en-us/p...	5/5/2021, 10:29 AM
Add a condition	Add a condition	https://docs.microsoft.com/en-us/p...	5/5/2021, 10:29 AM
Delete nodes - Design the topic's conversation...	Delete nodes - Design the topic's c...	https://docs.microsoft.com/en-us/p...	5/5/2021, 10:29 AM
Test and publish your bot	Test and publish your bot	https://docs.microsoft.com/en-us/p...	5/5/2021, 10:29 AM

Figure 9.4 – Topics generated from a source

7. You can now choose any of the topics, look at the content generated, and then from the option on the **Topics** record, you can select to add it to the list of available topics, as shown in the following screenshot:

Figure 9.5 – Add to Existing Topics

8. Your topics are now added to the **Existing** topics list, and you can choose to make edits and enable them when ready, as shown in the following screenshot:

Figure 9.6 – Enabling topics by setting the status to On

Now that we have seen how to introduce static data by generating topics from a data source, let's see next what the process to retrieve dynamic data from a data source is.

Working with dynamic data

The approach to working with dynamic data and reading it on demand is slightly different and involves running a Power Automate flow to retrieve data from the source system. We have seen a quick example of this in *Chapter 7, Building a Power Virtual Agents Application for Teams*. Overall, the process looks as presented in the following diagram:

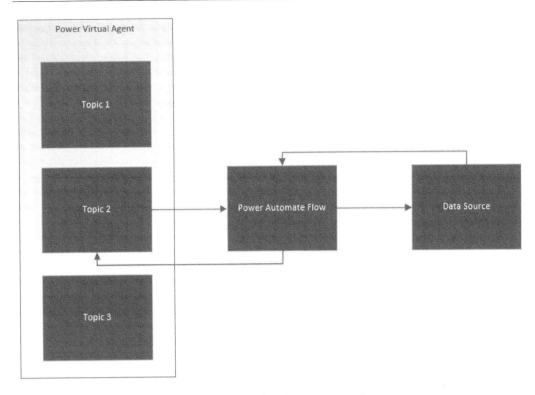

Figure 9.7 – Retrieving data from an external source

From within a topic, we call a **Power Automate flow**. That flow retrieves data from a data source, as configured, and the dataset is returned to the invoking topic to be presented in the conversation.

Let's see an example of building such a process next.

Retrieving data using available connectors

Using a Power Automate flow leverages a large set of available connectors to tap into external systems or data sources and retrieve various pieces of data to be returned to the conversation. There is a large number of available connectors, some created by Microsoft and others created by various vendors. If you cannot find an existing connector for your respective data source, you can always create a new custom connector. Depending on the data source, this could be either a simple configurable process, or it might require some more advanced custom coding.

In our example, we will use an existing Microsoft-provided connector to retrieve data from Dynamics 365 Sales and return to the conversation a set of active opportunity records. You can take a similar approach for any other tables in Dataverse, including standard tables such as Account or Contact if you are not using Dynamics 365 Sales. This example is a common scenario for organizations using a **Customer Relationship Management (CRM)** system.

Let's see how this is done:

1. We start by creating a new topic for our chatbot. I named this one `Sales` and created three trigger words for it, as shown in the following screenshot:

Figure 9.8 – Creating a Sales topic

2. Within this topic, I modified the first message to provide a clue as to what the scenario is, and then posed a question to determine the type of information the user will request. The following screenshot shows the **Question** configuration, as well as the two possible choice answers, **Opportunities** and **Leads**:

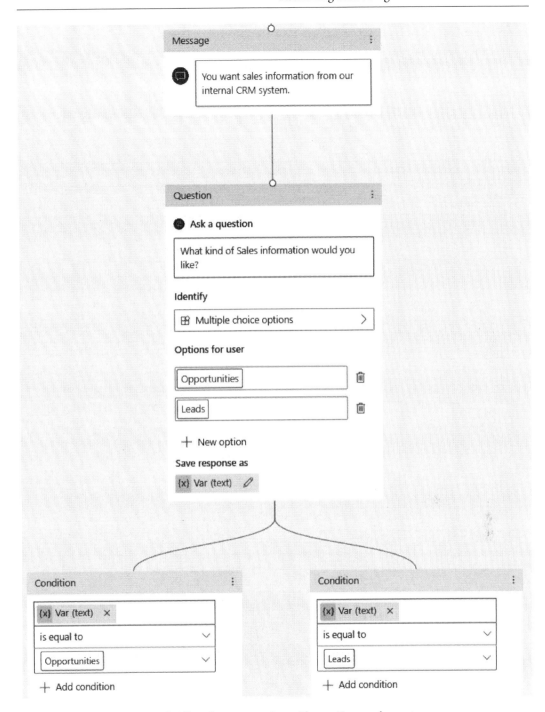

Figure 9.9 – Guiding the conversation with questions and preset answers

3. On the **Opportunities** condition, once the condition check is complete, we will call a Power Automate flow to retrieve opportunities from our Sales system. The action to trigger a flow is achieved by selecting the **Call an action** option and in the expanded window selecting **Create a flow**. Once your flow is created, you can select it directly as shown in the following screenshot, which presents the **Return Opportunities PVA Flow** that I created:

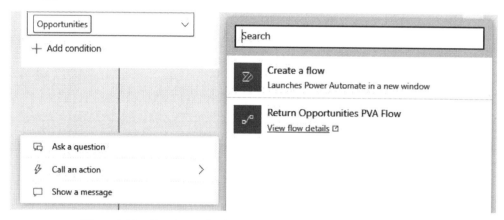

Figure 9.10 – Creating and selecting a Power Automate flow to trigger

4. Once you select the Power Automate flow, you can add a final message and set it to return the values retrieved by the flow. The setup looks as in the following screenshot:

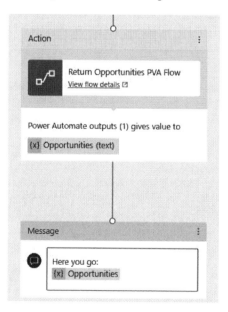

Figure 9.11 – Action and final message

5. With this setup in place, let's focus our attention on the Power Automate flow. When we chose to create it, Power Automate opened a new window to edit the new flow. We start with a power virtual agent trigger and a **Return value(s) to Power Virtual Agents** action at the end. We will need to fill in the blanks in between.

6. For the first step, right after the trigger, I want to declare a **String** variable to hold my response information. I will only present in a very simple way the names (titles) of each active opportunity in my Sales system. I will use the **Initialize variable** action and create a variable called `Opportunities` of the **String** type, as shown in the following screenshot:

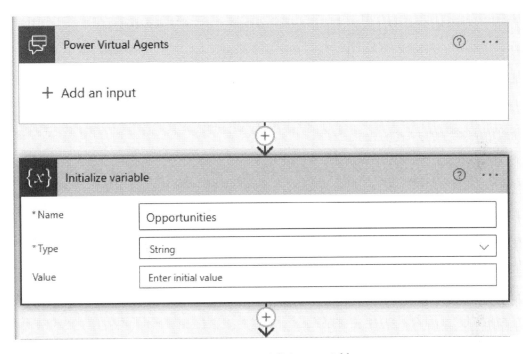

Figure 9.12 – Initializing a variable

7.   Next, I will make a call to my Sales system, and retrieve all active opportunities. You will want to use the **Microsoft Dataverse** connector, and find the **List rows** action, as shown in the following screenshot:

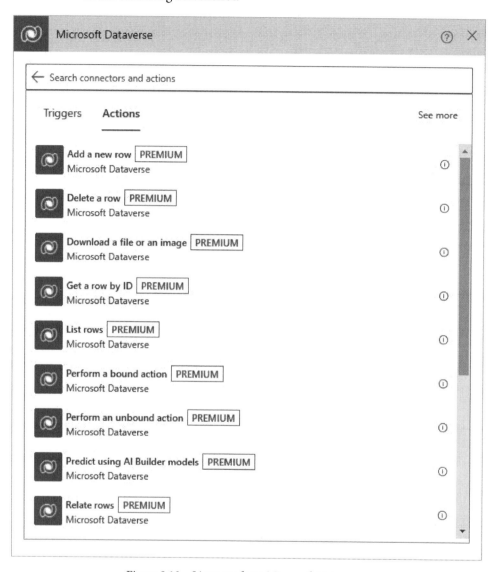

Figure 9.13 – List rows from Microsoft Dataverse

8.   Once you create the **List rows** card, you need to configure a few properties. First off, let's start by renaming the action to something that makes more sense. You do this by selecting the ellipsis at the top right and choosing **Rename**. I called it List Opportunities, as seen in the following screenshot:

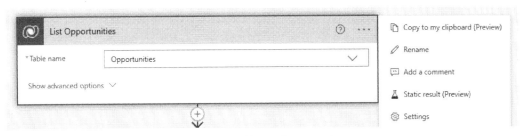

Figure 9.14 – Renaming an action

9. For **Table name**, I selected **Opportunities**, since this is what I intend to retrieve.

10. If you expand the **Show advanced options** area, you will see a set of additional configurations. I have used **Fetch Xml Query** here to retrieve the top 50 opportunities with a status of active, as seen in the following screenshot:

Figure 9.15 – Configuring additional properties for the query

11. The best way to generate such a query, if you are not familiar with the syntax, is to use a community tool such as **FetchXML Builder**, which is part of **XrmToolBox**, available at `https://www.xrmtoolbox.com/`.

12. With the query in place, next we need to loop through each of the returned records. We select the **Apply to each Control** action, as shown in the following screenshot:

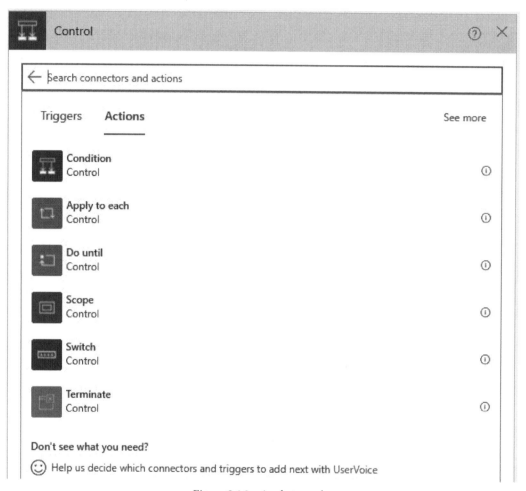

Figure 9.16 – Apply to each

13. We will rename this step `Loop through Opportunities`, and in the previous step output selection field, we will populate under **Dynamic content** the value of the previous step, as shown in the following screenshot:

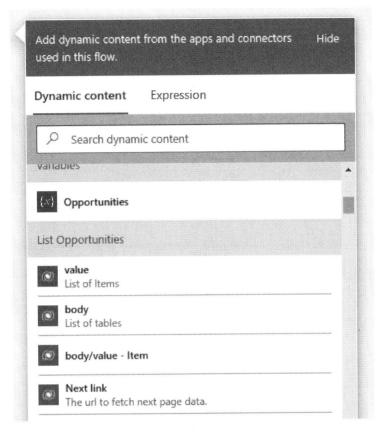

Figure 9.17 – Dynamic content value of List Opportunities

14. Finally, within the **Loop through Opportunities** step, we will add a new **Append to string variable** action. Within its properties, we first select the already-defined variable we called **Opportunities**, and the value to be appended is the topic of the **List Opportunities** step. This is the title of each opportunity record in our Sales system. The configuration looks as in the following screenshot:

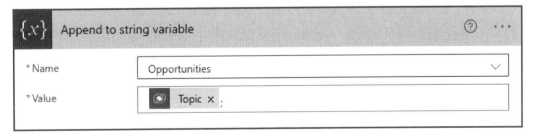

Figure 9.18 – Append to string variable

15. Finally, you complete the **Loop through Opportunities** step, which will look as in the following screenshot:

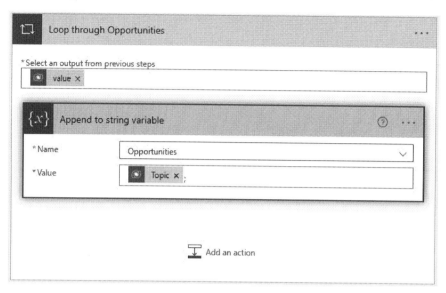

Figure 9.19 – Loop through Opportunities step configuration

16. Once this step is executed, the value of our temporary variable will include a list of all opportunity names, separated by a semicolon, as we defined the format. You can of course change how this is displayed, of the information you want to return. For example, you might want to consider returning the opportunity name, along with the total estimated revenue, or any other piece of information you are capturing in your Sales application regarding opportunities.

17. Finally, the last step of this process is to return this value to the Power Virtual Agent. We do this by filling in the details on the **Return value(s) to Power Virtual Agents** step. We will provide here a text type return, give it the name Opportunities, and select the variable we populated during the flow execution as the return value. The following screenshot shows this configuration:

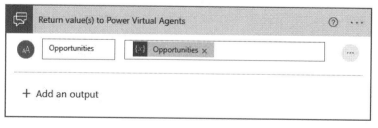

Figure 9.20 – Return value(s) to Power Virtual Agents

18. All you have remaining is to give this Power Automate flow a name and save it. You do this by selecting the default name at the top of the editor and providing your own custom name. I named this one `Return Opportunities PVA Flow`, as seen in the following screenshot:

Figure 9.21 – Giving the flow a name and saving

19. You can now close the Power Automate flow editor and return to your Power Virtual Agents editor.

We can now test the chatbot functionality. Let's do the following:

1. In the **Test bot** window, trigger the topic by typing `Sales`. The bot will respond with a question regarding the data to be retrieved, as seen in the following screenshot:

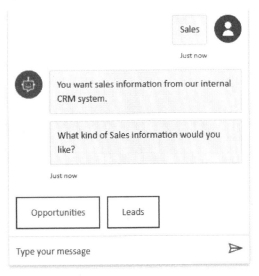

Figure 9.22 – Triggering the chatbot

2. Select **Opportunities** to retrieve the information from our Sales system. After a moment of execution, results are returned, as seen in the following screenshot:

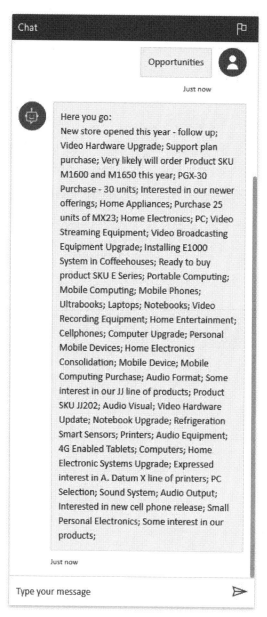

Figure 9.23 – Returning opportunities from the Sales system

3. Now you are ready to expand on the functionality if needed and publish this chatbot to either Teams or a public site.

Of course, you could now look at the functionality and determine that you should probably make some more enhancements. For one, you might want to return only opportunities related to the current user requesting this information. In addition, you might want to change the information returned, return links to each opportunity, or make other changes you can think of. I will leave this to you to play around with. This is only a simple example showing the power of leveraging Power Automate flows and connectors.

Next, let's look at what other data sources we can tap into.

Retrieving data from other sources

As mentioned before in this chapter, Power Automate provides a large number of connectors from both Microsoft as well as other third parties. Going to the Power Automate editor and selecting **Connectors** from the side navigation, we are presented with a list, as seen in the following screenshot:

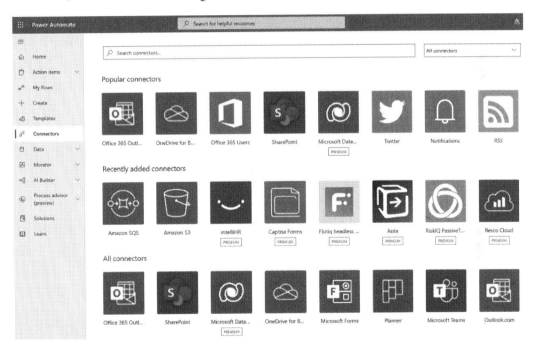

Figure 9.24 – Power Automate Connectors

You can use the search function to look for a connector to the application you want to retrieve data from. You will find two types of connectors available:

- **Regular connectors**: Connectors you can leverage with a standard Microsoft 365 license

- **Premium connectors**: Connectors available with a specific license, at an additional cost

If the application you want to interact with does not have a connector already available, you can create your own connectors. You can have these available only within your organization, or you can publish them to make them available to a wider audience. The publishing process takes you through additional approval steps. When making a connector available only within your organization, the approval process is limited to your organization's processes and best practices. Opposite to that, when publishing to the marketplace, the approval process also involves Microsoft, as they review and provide suggestions before approving a connector in the public marketplace.

For most organizations, when leveraging existing legacy applications, custom connectors will only be published within the organization.

Summary

In this chapter, we looked at surfacing data into our chatbot from a public page and from an external system. For the purpose of the second example provided, we leveraged the Dynamics 365 Sales application available in the same environment as the Power Virtual Agent. This allowed us to retrieve and present in the conversation a listing of available opportunity records.

In the next chapter, we will focus on some aspects of governance. We will look at both agents for the web as well as agents for Teams. We will investigate the approach to governance, some aspects to consider, as well as the most common governance scenarios.

Section 4:
Best Practices for
Power Virtual Agents

In this section, you will start to understand the broader considerations when planning and implementing Virtual Agents.

This section contains the following chapters:

- *Chapter 10, Power Virtual Agents Governance*
- *Chapter 11, Power Virtual Agents Best Practices*
- *Chapter 12, Power Virtual Agents Administration*

10
Power Virtual Agents Governance

In the previous chapters, we looked at building smart Power Virtual Agents chatbots for both the web as well as Teams. We gained enough experience to get started in this area. We can create agents that not only maintain a conversation but also guide the conversation and retrieve data from various sources to be included in the conversation.

The focus here will be on laying down the groundwork for how our environments will be set up and managed. We will look at several places where we get some good visibility into how our environments thrive, and where we look to determine whether any intervention is needed.

These last chapters will focus more on the general maintenance of agents.

In this chapter, our attention turns to governance. We will be looking at the following topics:

- General governance considerations
- Governance of Power Virtual Agents for the web
- Governance of Power Virtual Agents for Teams

At the end of this chapter, we should have a good understanding of how governance works for Power Virtual Agents, what some of the aspects we need to consider are, as well as differences between agents for the web or for Teams.

With that being said, let's get going. We will get started with general considerations.

General governance considerations

First off, you might ask: *What is governance?*

From an organization perspective, governance defines terms by which an organization controls processes and operates its business, as well as the ways in which accountability is defined. This typically includes issues around ethics, risk management, compliance, and administration.

In this chapter, we want to focus primarily on aspects of platform governance, and how accountability for the solutions provided is assigned. We will also look at aspects of ethics, risk management, and compliance, and how these impact our design and deployment.

Along with the life cycle of our application in an environment, we will look at the considerations for building your first Power Virtual Agents chatbot, monitoring its usage, engaging the community for feedback, regular environment management, as well as some aspects of tenant and environment hygiene.

There's a lot, so let's start by breaking it down into several categories:

- Governance in the context of the entire Power Platform
- Security management
- Monitoring approach
- Application(s) management
- Tenant, environment, and application hygiene

Let's look at each one of these categories in detail.

Governance in the context of the entire Power Platform

When it comes to governance, Microsoft provides robust tools at the Power Platform level we can leverage. The entire Power Platform is comprised of the following major services:

- Power BI for dashboarding, visualization, and reporting

- Power Apps for no-code or low-code application creation

- Power Automate for workflow automation, including both cloud and desktop flows

- Power Virtual Agents as the bot creation solution

In addition, the following supporting services feed and augment the platform capabilities:

- Dataverse for data storage and business logic

- Data connectors for internal-external data access

- AI Builder for intelligence on applications and business flows

The entire platform spans and integrates with major offerings including **Microsoft 365**, **Microsoft Azure**, and **Dynamics 365**.

Let's next look at security concerns.

Security management

When we begin our tenant setup, and throughout the life of the environment, security is one of the most important aspects to consider. We begin a tenant setup with actions to define and secure the foundations. Here, we look at access permissions and security roles.

As such, a lot of the administrative tools are shared with offerings such as Microsoft 365 and Azure. For example, user account management can be handled through the Office 365 admin console, which is powered by Azure Active Directory. For advanced administration, you can perform the same and more complex actions directly through the Azure Active Directory administration.

This is typically achieved by the IT team. As a citizen developer or pro developer, you will work with IT to request and leverage the proper environment and configuration for your applications. Remember how in *Chapter 8, Integrating the Power Virtual Agent into Teams*, we leveraged the users already authenticated on the platform. Or look back at *Chapter 6, Handling Authentication and Personalization*, where we first authenticated a user to provide them with personalized information. This is all achievable through leveraging mechanisms already in place and supported through security management.

Some of the essential capabilities around security that require analysis and planning include items such as the following:

- Securing access to the tenant, environment, resources, and applications.

- Securing individual environments, with consideration for both external access as well as access between environments. This includes limiting access to specific resources, data, and connectors.

- Securing and protecting the information within each tenant and environment.

All these aspects require planning and a robust strategy for both the initial rollout as well as the ongoing maintenance.

Data Loss Prevention (**DLP**) allows the creation of specific policies to restrict access to various environment elements. Here, you restrict access to connectors that have the potential to leak corporate information externally. For certain connectors, you could go to the individual actions on a connector, thus maybe allowing certain connectors for ingesting data but not leaking any of the internal data externally:

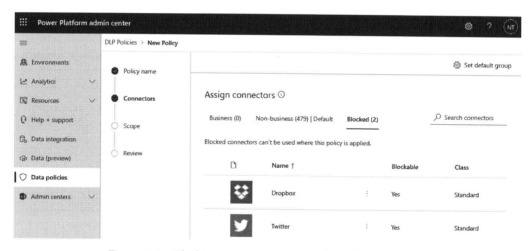

Figure 10.1 – Blocking access to connectors through DLP policies

Once you have your tenant and environment created and configured, the next step is to create a plan for ongoing monitoring.

Monitoring approach

For application monitoring, Microsoft has built a set of analytical capabilities meant to make our life easier. Of course, we are not limited to the provided tools, and we can extend those capabilities with our own sets of analysis and reporting capabilities.

These default capabilities are continuously revised and extended based on community feedback.

When talking about an approach to monitoring, some of the aspects we must plan include the following:

- The availability and usage of the out-of-the-box analytics capabilities.

- Custom analytics capabilities built to extend the out-of-the-box features. These could be both long-term solutions as well as more ad hoc solutions to serve an urgent but time-bound need.

- Auditing and logging in order to create a historical trace.

Monitoring capabilities introduced in the Power Platform Admin center include the ability to see overall capacity usage, as shown in the following screenshot:

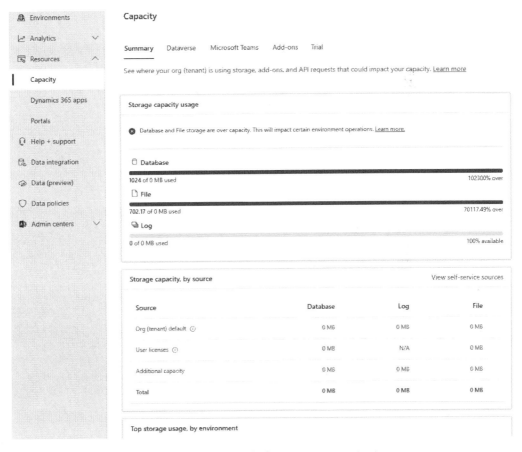

Figure 10.2 – Power Platform capacity monitoring

In addition, you can drill down into one of the environments in your tenant, and see reporting on database, file, and log usage, as shown in the following screenshot:

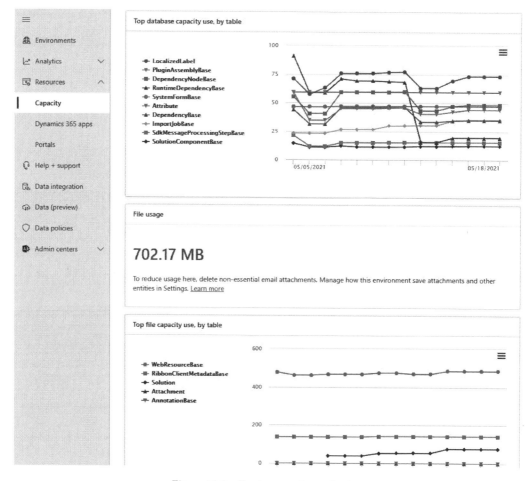

Figure 10.3 – Environment monitoring

Next, let's see how we can drill down and look at application management.

Application(s) management

When it comes to the ongoing management of tenants, environments, and applications, again we find some solutions and capabilities provided by Microsoft. These include the following:

- **Power Platform Center of Excellence** (**CoE**) – a custom solution provided free to simplify monitoring and reporting

- **Application Lifecycle Management** (**ALM**) and automation capabilities around ALM
- Training resources available free of charge

In addition, capabilities can be built to enhance these solutions.

Some of the most important information you will be monitoring is application popularity in usage, for both personal productivity and organizational applications. You will be able to quickly determine when applications pick up in popularity and should be promoted from personal productivity apps into organizational apps. The reverse is also true, where you can determine the end of life for specific applications based on drops in usage.

This leads right into tenant, environment, and application hygiene.

Tenant, environment, and application hygiene

In this category, we primarily look at keeping things organized and active. We plan and monitor for orphaned and unused applications and components, and we archive and delete them as per the governance plans in place. Our planning should define the standard for what we consider minimal usage, and when an application, environment, or tenant is ready to be retired, as well as the actions required to achieve this result.

But let's focus more specifically on Power Virtual Agents and start with Power Virtual Agents for the web.

Governance of Power Virtual Agents for the web

When working with chatbots for the web, there are a few important items to monitor for:

- Monitor usage to determine how often your chatbot is called.
- Monitor usage and data occupied by chat logs.
- Determine retention policies for the chat log data.

You can begin the monitoring of activities from the chatbot editor by choosing the bot **Analytics** option on the navigation. The categories available include the following:

- **Summary** presents the total number of sessions over a period of time, the engagement and resolution rates, escalations and abandonments, along with other metrics. The following screenshot shows this dashboard:

Figure 10.4 – Power Virtual Agents Analytics Summary dashboard

- In addition, if configured to capture **Customer Satisfaction**, you can report on it, along with session information and billing details. This will allow you to make decisions around improving the chatbot functionality; adding, removing, or updating topics; and other details.

To look at chat logs, you need to export the chatlog data from the Power Platform maker portal available at `https://make.powerapps.com`, by going to **Data | Tables**, expanding the **Data** menu on the top ribbon, selecting **Export data**, and finding and selecting **ConversationTranscript** as shown in the following screenshot:

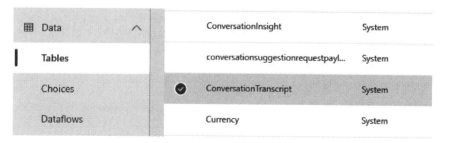

Figure 10.5 – Export ConversationTranscript

Finally, to configure a retention policy, you need to do that from the Power Platform maker portal, by selecting the **Settings** icon on the top-right side of the screen and choosing **Advanced Settings**. Navigate to **Settings | Data Management | Bulk Record Deletion** as seen in the following screenshot:

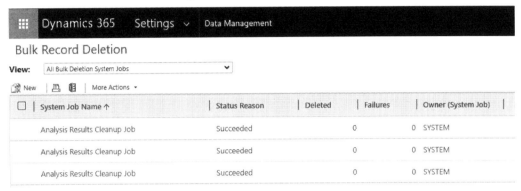

Figure 10.6 – Bulk Record Deletion jobs

Here, you create a new rule to delete records older than a certain duration, as determined by your organization's policies and standards. The following screenshot shows such a rule defined:

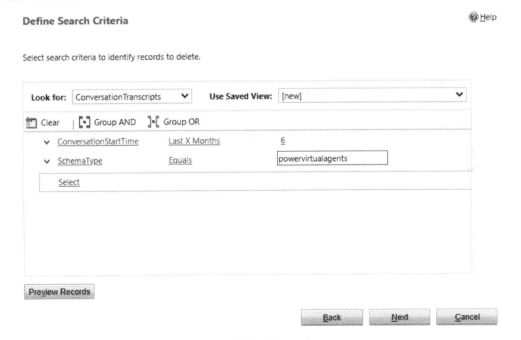

Figure 10.7 – Bulk delete rule settings

Let's see next what some of the differences are when creating chatbots for Teams.

Governance of Power Virtual Agents for Teams

When working with Power Virtual Agents for Teams, a similar set of analytics is available from the chatbot editor. You can get a **Summary** of information, along with **Customer Satisfaction**, **Sessions**, and **Billing** details.

An important aspect to consider is the **DLP** settings, allowing or blocking the specific connectors the user triggered in the Power Automate flows from within your chatbot. If you are presenting a chatbot that calls a flow using a connector deemed unsafe and blocked through DLP, you will not get any results.

Another aspect to consider and plan for is the rollout of your agent. If you remember from *Chapter 7, Building a Power Virtual Agents Application for Teams*, we did have to select a team right from the creation wizard, as shown in the following screenshot:

Figure 10.8 – Select a team for the chatbot

When planning your chatbot for Teams, always consider what the appropriate team is for your chatbot. You can see the deployed chatbots by team, as shown in the following screenshot:

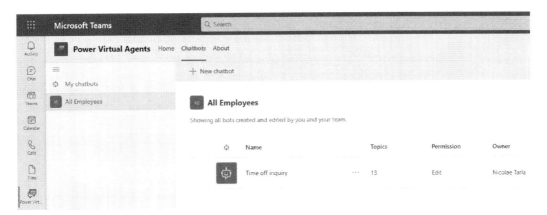

Figure 10.9 – Chatbots by Team

Do keep in mind that when publishing a chatbot in Teams, you need to provide the following information:

- A link to a privacy statement
- A link to the terms of use for the chatbot
- A link to the developer's website
- The developer's name

While Microsoft provides default templates for these, part of the deployment process should include updating these templates with the relevant information.

Summary

In this chapter, we looked at general governance considerations and specific details for agents for the web and Teams. The most common considerations were brought forward, and you should now have a pretty good idea of the considerations when preparing a governance plan.

In the next chapter, we will focus on best practices. We will look at design, implementation, and management aspects, as well as some of the common dos and don'ts.

11
Power Virtual Agents Best Practices

In previous chapters, we looked at some of the governance considerations around using Power Virtual Agents for both the web as well as Teams. We then looked at some aspects specific to either the web or Teams creation and deployment options.

In this chapter, we want to look at some best practices. When performing certain configurations, it is always a good idea to follow specific patterns and best practices. This enhances the ability to maintain your products in a more consistent manner and creates a certain level of familiarity within the organization. Besides the standard platform best practices, your organization could set its own set of rules and best practices to enhance the standard platform best practices. We will be reviewing the following items:

- Design and build best practices
- Implementing best practices
- Managing best practices

By the end of this chapter, we should have a good understanding of considerations and approaches for creating new Power Virtual Agents or refactoring existing ones.

But let's delve right into it.

Design and build best practices

Historically, bots have been hard to create, as well as expensive to maintain. While the no-code approach mitigates some of these circumstances, we should not forget that a simplified interface for bot creation does not suddenly make it easy and cheap.

Putting together the right team

The difficulty in creating chatbots, while reduced from a technical perspective, still has some significant challenges. The creation of chatbots requires a blend of knowledge from subject matter experts and know-how from developers. As such, one important challenge remains. The communication across domains must be smooth for best results. Technical experts provide added value by finding the best approach to meet the needs of the business. But building something highly technical just for the sake of tech will end up in failure. As such, begin your journey by putting together the right team, with the right balance of business know-how, subject matter experts, along with developers and technical experts. Throw in the mix someone with some behavioral expertise and you increase your chance of success exponentially. Thus, obviously, the following stands:

For best results, put together the right team.

Providing measurable value

For a chatbot to be successful, it must provide value. While simple conversations can easily be created, they can only cover so much before it becomes obvious that it is just a machine responding to simple queries.

We are not trying to create a chatbot that will pass the Turing test here, or a full AI. But we must strike a balance between a simple FAQ we can just read on a page and the feeling of something a little smarter than that. As such, the chatbot must not only provide information as preconfigured through simplistic responses, but it must also be able to retrieve data and provide personalized responses. As such, the following applies:

Bots provide added value by integrating with backend systems and provide personalized answers.

Power Virtual Agents life cycle

The Power Virtual Agents platform allows an organization to provide value through the ability to create natural engaging experiences. It allows chatbot owners to continuously enhance their products. It adds the ability to integrate with simple AI-driven processes as well as backend systems, to not only retrieve and provide personalized user interactions but also take and perform actions.

As part of the ongoing continuous enhancements, a complete life cycle includes the following stages:

- **Creation of a simple chatbot**: Here we generate the first version of our chatbot.

- **Leverage starter topics**: Get familiar with the starter topics available with bot creation.

- **Author and enhance topics**: Create the necessary topics to reflect the business needs.

- **Integrate chatbot with backend systems**: Leverage a custom **Application Programming Interface (API)** using Microsoft Power Automate flows to integrate with external systems.

- **Extend chatbot with custom skills**: Create skills for custom scenarios.

- **Publish chatbot to channels**: Present the chatbot to the intended audiences.

- **Monitor the chatbot**: Keep track of performance and statistics and take actions to improve based on the captured data.

- **Enhance the chatbot**: Build on top of the existing functionality by correcting or adding new features.

This repetitive process is called the **Power Virtual Agents life cycle**, as depicted in the following diagram:

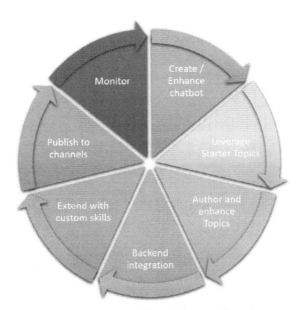

Figure 11.1 – Power Virtual Agents life cycle

Understanding your licensing constraints

When working with Power Virtual Agents, make sure you know the licenses you have and what you can do within the confinements of that license. The behavior is different between chatbots for the web and for Teams. Within Teams, the Microsoft 365 license covers deploying chatbot to Teams only, while the Power Virtual Agents license supports all channels. Also, depending on the license, you will have access to either only standard connectors with a Microsoft 365 license or premium connectors with a Power Virtual Agents license.

When creating more advanced chatbots leveraging the custom Microsoft Bot Framework along with its dialogs functionality, you must have a Power Virtual Agents subscription.

As such, make sure your chatbot design takes into consideration the expected licensing model for your final product.

Handing off to support agents

When designing your chatbot functionality, along with the capability to hand off to a live agent, take into consideration several aspects, including the following:

- **The technical ability to support the handoff**: How and where the agents will receive the handoff. Typically, this is done in a customer support application and requires some level of integration.

- **The expected volumes of handoff**: You do not want to suddenly create an overflow of support requests coming into your support team. While these numbers can be estimated during the design process, they must be reviewed on an ongoing basis and adjustments should be made to the bot or the team.

Defining the success factors to monitor for

A chatbot offered for support can only be successful if it provides real value to its users. There are several considerations when designing for success:

- **Know your customer**: Understand the needs and the expected scenarios you intend to resolve through this functionality.

- **Understand the request and relate it to the correct topic**: This includes planning key phrases, as well as defining the current conversation path based on the responses received. This is usually a lot easier when you guide the conversation with predefined responses rather than trying to interpret freeform responses. It is imperative to understand how AI uses the natural language for parsing input for trigger phrases.

- **Provide accurate, latest, and most relevant content**: Review the content at timed intervals and put into place processes that include the chatbot review when support materials are being updated.

- **Provide a personalized experience by integrating with core supporting systems and providing context-aware responses**: Part of such experiences could also include the ability to take actions for users based on the conversation.

- **Plan for a smooth handoff to a support person**: Create a smooth experience for the user, by avoiding abrupt changes in the conversation.

Taking into consideration these aspects, the entire user experience will be greatly enhanced, resulting in a much more successful implementation and operation.

This leads to the next best practice.

Alignment with organization goals

More than anything, when deciding to provide to users this type of new channel, you must have a valid reason for it. In most circumstances, this arises out of a need to handle repetitive requests for the same information and has the final goal of reducing the workload on existing support staff as well as providing faster answers to users. This will help in the following aspects:

- Reduce the volume of calls for support

- Improve performance indicators

When providing this functionality to external users through a channel such as a support portal, for example, you could also look at branding implications, as well as **Customer Satisfaction (CSAT)**.

Managing your starter template

While the platform created your chatbots with some starter components, including the **Lessons** topics, make sure to disable and delete all unwanted elements. Lessons are there for guidance and to help with the learning process. Do not leave them in the final product. It is not enough to just disable those topics, but you should delete them altogether.

Understanding the environments

By default, chatbots get created in the default Power Platform environment. You should change the environment during creation by selecting the **More Options** action and choosing the correct environment. This way, all your creator teams' chatbots are grouped in the correct environment and easier to manage. These chatbots are only visible in the environment where they are created, so make sure the users accessing these chatbots for testing as well as the final users are pointed to the correct environment.

Let's have a look next at some best practices for implementation.

Implementing best practices

Once planning is complete, we can start creating our chatbots. When doing so, there are some considerations that will make our life a lot easier.

Let's review some of these.

Starting small and building up

When implementing a chatbot for the first time, take a pilot approach. Create a bot with a smaller footprint, a reduced number of topics, and a smaller target audience. Monitor its usage during the pilot and identify a selected mix of simple and advanced topics that provide the most success. Then look at ways to improve and build on that to create a more robust offering.

As you expose the chatbot to a larger audience, you now have a framework of items to monitor for, as well as a defined approach to pushing enhancements.

Creation of the first bot versus additional bots

When you create your first chatbot, make sure to select the correct environment during the creation process.

On the creation of additional chatbots, it will be easier to recognize the correct environment based on elements already existing in that environment.

Topics structured around one unit of conversation

To simplify the management of chatbots, it is advisable to structure them around distinct units of conversation. Trying to jam multiple conversation scenarios into a single chatbot will only result in more complex logic and increased challenges when maintaining and upgrading the functionality. Following a "keep it simple" approach, make sure your chatbots are structured around distinct units of conversation.

Writing topic trigger phrases

When writing trigger phrases, there are a few things you can do to improve success. These include things such as the following:

- **Follow a conversational topic**: Use a regular speech pattern rather than being abstract.

- **Do not be too verbose**: Be brief and concise when creating trigger phrases.

- **Create friendly conversations**: Assume a user will not have the same technical vocabulary as a developer.

Setting the expectations

It is good practice to let the user know from the beginning that they are interacting with a chatbot and not a real user. Equally important is to set the expectation from the greeting to create a level of comfort. For example, you might start with a statement such as the following:

Hi there, my name is Jane, and I am a chatbot. I can help you today with information on schedules, orders, and returns.

Such a statement sets the stage for a more meaningful conversation.

Asking questions

When interacting with a user, it is not always about providing answers. To keep the discussion flowing, questions are a great part of the conversation.

We have seen in various examples the ability to guide the user by providing a subset of possible answers. That is a great approach, but it does not always work. Sometimes you need to ask a question.

When phrasing your questions, never use open-ended questions. By phrasing the questions correctly, you will narrow down the scope of the conversation, expect a more specific and identifiable answer, as well as providing clues to the user as to the type of answer the chatbot expects to receive.

Handling long-running processes

While for simple conversations a chatbot can respond almost instantly, there are instances when the conversation will take longer. Always provide the user with a visual clue as to the fact that the process is still ongoing. Just like talking to a person and seeing through visual clues that they are thinking about the answer they will provide, provide a similar clue through the use of messages. A chatbot that needs to retrieve order information might pop up a message stating the following:

I will go ahead and retrieve your order information now. This might take a moment.

This way, a user can expect to wait a moment longer than usual.

Let's see some standard best practices for managing our chatbots next.

Managing best practices

Once you have a chatbot released, it is imperative to manage and maintain its performance, as well as monitoring for improvements. The following best practices apply to the ongoing management of chatbots postproduction.

Reviewing analytics for continuous improvements

Once you launch a chatbot, you should be monitoring its performance closely. This way, you can determine whether it is meeting your performance indicators and success metrics. Through continuous monitoring, you can identify and act upon opportunities for improvement.

The chatbot analytics tell a good story. We can start from the **Summary** dashboard, which presents information around sessions, engagement, escalation, resolution and abandon rates, CSAT, as well as outcomes over time. This is presented in the following screenshot:

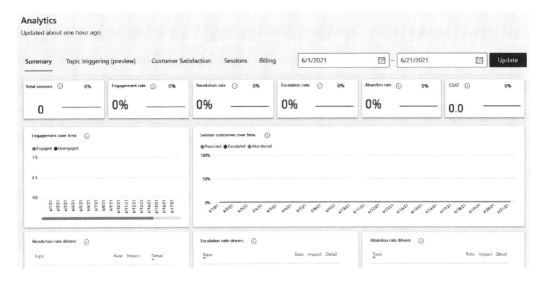

Figure 11.2 – Summary dashboard

A newer addition to the analytics is the ability to analyze topic triggers, with details on **Overlap detection** where we look at similarities between trigger phases, as well as suggestions on new topics based on existing user inputs. These are all AI-driven capabilities, and must be enabled in the **Settings** area, as shown in the following screenshot:

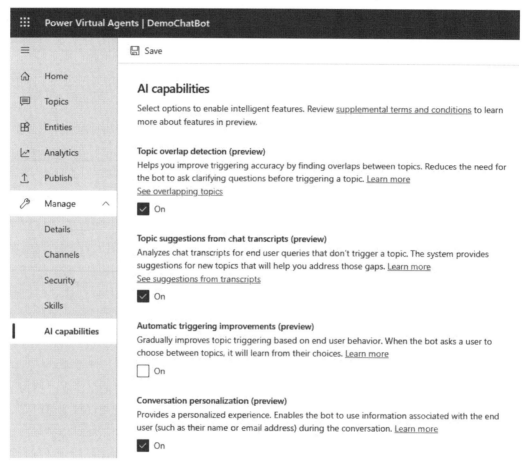

Figure 11.3 – Enabling AI capabilities

Once these features are enabled, they are presented in a dashboard as in the following screenshot. You can act upon any of these suggestions to make improvements to your existing chatbot:

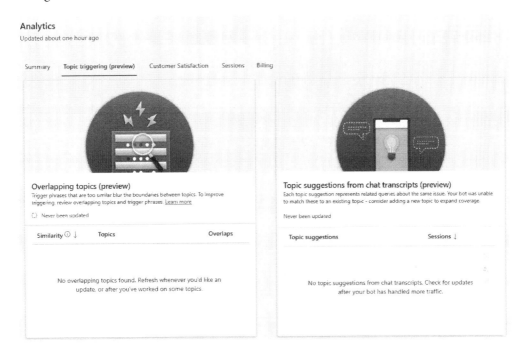

Figure 11.4 – Topic triggering AI capabilities

The **Customer Satisfaction** dashboard presents overall satisfaction based on the ratings provided by users.

Finally, **Sessions** and **Billing** provide you with the ability to download sessions and see details around the costs associated with running your chatbot.

The out-of-the-box-provided dashboards are great ways to inform an administrator whether the interacting customers are satisfied with the service or not. Seeing high abandon rates and escalation rates of negative CSAT results means you need to go back to the drawing board and find better ways to service your customers. This could be as simple as adding new topics or adjusting existing topics, finding better escalation points, or identifying other scenarios that require improvements.

Deleting bots

When a chatbot has outlived its expected lifetime, it is time for cleanup. This could be part of a regular cleanup and maintenance routine, at fixed timed intervals, or part of the chatbot-defined life cycle. For example, if we create a chatbot to provide information about a conference, it becomes obsolete once the conference has ended.

Always delete bots that have outlived their usefulness. You delete a chatbot by removing it from your environment. You access this functionality from the chatbot editor interface, by selecting the cog icon at the top-right side of the screen, and selecting the **General settings** option, as demonstrated in the following screenshot:

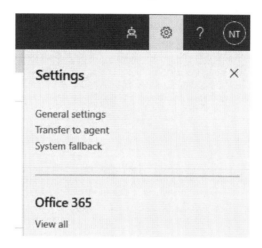

Figure 11.5 – General settings

This brings forward an overlay **Settings** form, as shown in the following screenshot:

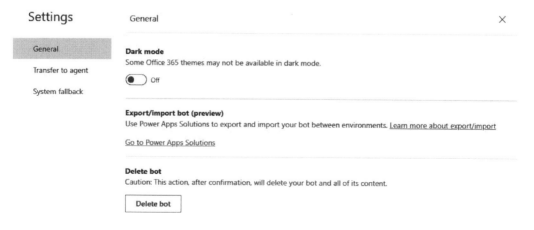

Figure 11.6 – Settings overlay and Delete bot option

On the **General** tab, we find the **Delete bot** button. Clicking this allows us to remove the chatbot from our environment. For confirmation, you are prompted to type in the name of your chatbot.

If you are working in an environment where licenses have expired, you can still remove the chatbots by selecting the option to permanently delete your bots.

Known issues and working around them

At the time of writing, Microsoft has published several known issues and solutions for them:

- Insufficient permissions will result in the **You do not have permissions to any environments. Please get access from an administrator** message. If you receive this message and have the necessary permissions, it simply means you do not have an environment for Power Virtual Agents created. Create a new environment and use that environment to create your chatbot.

- An environment does not show in the list of available environments. This is common in the following situations:

  You do not have a database created in the respective environment. You must first create a database in the environment before creating your first chatbot.

  The environment is created in a region that does not support this functionality. While great strides are made to offer similar functionality in all regions, some discrepancies exist due to either staggered rollouts or missing infrastructure for certain services. You must create an environment in a region that supports this functionality. Look up the Microsoft documentation to find out whether the region you selected supports this functionality.

Summary

In this chapter, we looked at some of the most common best practices when working with Power Virtual Agents. We reviewed the design, build, implementation, and post-implementation management aspects, as we now understand how and why certain decisions are made with regard to Power Virtual Agents.

In the next and final chapter, we will delve a little deeper into the administration aspect for Power Virtual Agents and focus our attention primarily on the post-implementation maintenance and troubleshooting aspects. See you there.

12

Power Virtual Agents Administration

Previous chapters presented some of the most common best practices when designing, implementing, and managing Power Virtual Agents.

In this final chapter of this book, we want to tackle the administration aspects of Power Virtual Agents. We will look at basic management principles, as well as monitoring and collecting data about usage and possible improvements we can make to our existing agents' logic and functionality. It is important to monitor, observe, and improve our virtual agents in order to provide better services to our customers. We will be reviewing the following aspects:

- Managing Power Virtual Agents
- Enabling and disabling Power Virtual Agents
- Modifying Power Virtual Agents
- Monitoring the success of Power Virtual Agents
- Troubleshooting issues

Along with the previous two chapters, we should gain a solid foundation on the process of designing, monitoring, and enhancing the functionality of our chatbots that will put us on the path to success.

Let's talk about administration.

Managing Power Virtual Agents

As part of the management process for our Power Virtual Agents, we need to understand and work with the following concepts:

- Working with environments
- Data locations for organizations
- Assigning and managing licenses

We will look at each one of these aspects in detail next.

Working with environments

The Power Virtual Agents platform allows us to create and manage chatbots in different environments, as well as switching between these environments.

An environment allows you to store and share a segmented section of your organization's business data along with a chatbot. You group these elements, along with applications and flows, to create full line-of-business solutions. In addition to that, you configure security rules for environments, allowing you to define who can access which data and processes.

Typically, when creating and managing environments, you define the segmentation based on your organization structure, such as by department, or for larger organizations you could segment by geographical location. You could have a combination of both, where you create environments by country for a multi-national organization as well as by department within each geographical branch.

The environment creation and management are handled from the Power Platform admin portal, and it applies to Power Virtual Agents as well as other Power Platform services, including Power Apps and Power Automate.

You can access the Power Platform admin portal at the following link:

`https://admin.powerplatform.com`

You sign in with an admin account, and on the **Environments** tab, you will find a listing of current environments as well as the ability to create new environments and manage existing ones, as presented in the following screenshot:

Figure 12.1 – Environments listing

When creating a new environment, you must specify the following details:

- **An environment name**: You will typically follow a standard across your organization for naming environments.

- **The environment type**: This includes options such as **Production**, **Sandbox**, or **Trial**.

- **The region in which the environment will be hosted**: Note that this cannot be changed later. You should select the region closest to where most of the service users will be located and that provides the features you are looking for.

- **Purpose**: This is not a required field, but as a good practice, you should provide a description here.

- **Create a database for this environment**: For Power Virtual Agents, you must create a database. You can do this on this step, or you can do it later after the environment is created. You must have the database created before you can start creating chatbots.

The following screenshot shows the environment creation window:

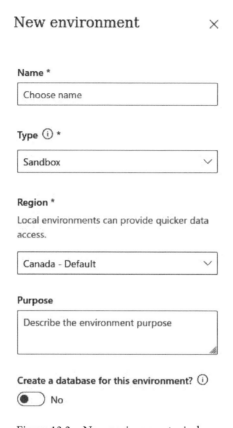

Figure 12.2 – New environment window

With an environment created, you are now ready to start creating chatbots.

Data locations for organizations

As mentioned previously, choosing a data location for your environment is especially important, and cannot be modified later. For transferring an environment to a new geographical location, you must create a new environment in that new region and migrate your data and configurations. This can be a very time-consuming process, depending on the complexity of deployed applications and services. For this reason, it is imperative that you select the correct data location from the beginning.

The data location settings will dictate a few localization options, including the formatting of items such as dates and times, numbers, postal codes, and currency.

The platform supports the following formatting locales for the English language:

- **en-AU** for Australian English
- **en-CA** for Canadian English
- **en-GB** for British English
- **en-IN** for Indian English
- **en-US** for United States English

The data location is important as it decides the selection of data centers. These are also called regions. Within each region, there is replication as per the cloud design.

The following regions are currently available:

- **Asia Pacific** – including locations in Singapore and Hong Kong
- **Australia** – including locations in New South Wales and Victoria
- **Canada** – including locations in Toronto and Quebec City
- **Europe** – including locations in the Netherlands and Ireland
- **France** – including locations in Paris and Marseille
- **India** – including locations in Pune and Chennai
- **Japan** – including locations in Tokyo and Osaka
- **South America** – including locations in São Paulo, with replication in Texas
- **Switzerland** – including locations in Zurich and Geneva
- **United Kingdom** – including locations in London and Cardiff
- **United States** – including locations in Virginia, Iowa, and Washington

Microsoft will keep customer data in the region selected and will not transfer it outside of the selected region, with some exceptions.

Assigning and managing licenses

From a licensing perspective, when using the Power Virtual Agents web app, the users of your bot do not require a license. Anyone with access to the chatbot location can use the chatbot with no additional licensing requirements.

This is in contrast with Power Virtual Agents for Teams, where the users of your chatbot must be licensed for Teams.

When it comes to creating Power Virtual Agents, the users who will participate in the creation process must have a per-user license. This is a user license that allows creating and editing chatbots.

In addition to that, a tenant license is also required. This license is not assignable to users.

Both licenses can be purchased from the **Microsoft 365 admin center**, in the billing section, as seen in the following screenshot:

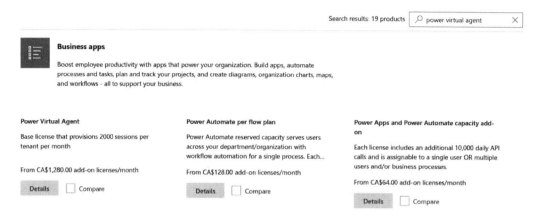

Figure 12.3 – Billing in the Microsoft 365 admin center

As a rule of thumb, you will acquire a tenant license, along with one or more per-user licenses. You can assign these per-user licenses to users, as well as reassigning them to other users when needed.

Let's see next how to work with Power Virtual Agents, in particular how to enable or disable them.

Enabling and disabling Power Virtual Agents

When working with chatbots, there are a few constraints we should be aware of. When reaching or exceeding these limits, the chatbot can stop normal functionality, resulting in unexpected interruptions for our customers. As such, these are items that must be monitored.

The imposed quotas by the platform are in place to protect the service from overloading or potentially crashing. These quotas and rate limits will throttle the service load.

When such occurrences happen, your chat conversation could return a message such as **Send failed. Retry**.

When working with Power Virtual Agents for Teams, you will have a limit of 50 chatbots per team. Also, on Power Virtual Agents for Web, you will have a limit of 1,000 topics per bot in Dataverse environments. These are just some examples; all details can be found in the Microsoft documentation available at the following link:

```
https://docs.microsoft.com/en-us/power-virtual-agents/
requirements-quotas
```

As your organization starts creating more chatbots with more complex functionality, you must monitor these limits.

As part of the standard administration functions, you will need to analyze the most commonly used chatbots and identify the ones with low usage or low performance or with high rates of escalation. When approaching limits, you will have to consider which chatbots are good candidates for disabling. As you enable new chatbots to launch new functionality, some of the old ones that are either outdated or do not produce the expected results should become good candidates to be disabled.

Let's have a look next at how to go about modifying existing Power Virtual Agents functionality in order to add value and remove fringe cases that are not that popular.

Modifying Power Virtual Agents

Once you have your chatbots deployed, your journey is just starting. You need to monitor for performance and continue to make incremental updates to better serve your customers.

When working with chatbots, just like any other custom solutions, you should be following a strict **Application Life Cycle Management** (**ALM**) process, as defined by your organization. In the case of Power Virtual Agents, one important component of this ALM process is the use of solutions. At a minimum, you will build your chatbots in a development environment, you will deploy to a test environment, and when approved, you will deploy to a production environment. You achieve this by packaging your customization in a solution. The solution is a container holding your configurations. It can include one or more chatbots, along with Power Automate flows and other components as needed. At a minimum, you will have at least one chatbot in a solution.

To create a solution for your chatbot, follow these steps:

1. Go to the top-right cog icon for settings, and select **General settings**, as shown in the following screenshot:

Figure 12.4 – General settings

2. On the **General** tab, you will find the **Export/import bot** option, with a link to **Power Apps Solutions**, as seen in the following screenshot:

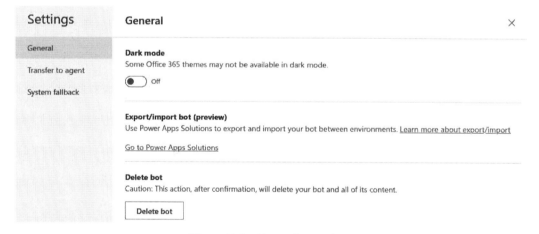

Figure 12.5 – Export/import bot

3. Click on **Go to Power Apps Solutions** and you are taken to the **Solutions** listing in your current environment. You can choose here from an existing solution to add the chatbot or create a new solution by selecting the **New solution** option on the ribbon. The following screenshot shows this screen:

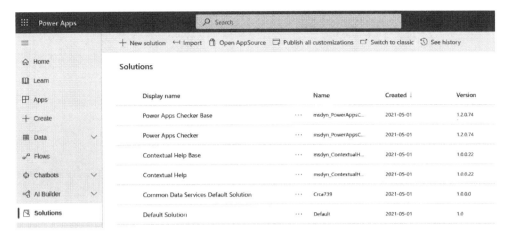

Figure 12.6 – Power Apps Solutions

4. When creating a new solution, you must define the solution display name and the internal name for the solution, create or select a publisher, and define the current version of the solution. The following screenshot shows the **New solution** screen:

Figure 12.7 – New solution screen

5. Once you select a solution, on the ribbon, select the **Add existing** option and choose **Chatbot** from the available options. On the screen that opens, select the chatbot you want to add to the solution, as shown in the following screenshot:

Add existing chatbots   ×

Select chatbots from other solutions or chatbots that aren't in solutions yet. Adding chatbots that aren't already in solutions will also add them to Common Data Service.

1 chatbot selected   🔎 Search chatbots

	Display name ∨	Name	Managed...	Owner	Status
●	DemoChatBot	DemoChatBot	🔒	Nicolae Tarla	-

Figure 12.8 – Selecting a chatbot to add to the solution

6. Click on **Add** when done. Your solution will refresh to show all the chatbot components added to your solution, as shown in the following screenshot:

Solutions > **My Chatbot Solution**

Display name ∨		Name	Type ∨	Managed...	Modified	Owner	Status
Call an action	···	Call an action	Topic	🔒	3 wk ago	Nicolae Tarla	-
Confirmed Failure	···	Confirmed Failure	Topic	🔒	3 wk ago	Nicolae Tarla	-
Confirmed Success	···	Confirmed Success	Topic	🔒	3 wk ago	Nicolae Tarla	-
Create and edit topics in your Power Virtual Agents bot	···	Create and edit topics in your Power Virtual Agents bc	Topic	🔒	3 wk ago	Nicolae Tarla	-
CSAT Rating	···	CSAT Rating	Bot entity	🔒	3 wk ago	Nicolae Tarla	-
DemoChatBot ⬈	···	DemoChatBot	Chatbot	🔒	5 d ago	Nicolae Tarla	-
End of Conversation	···	End of Conversation	Topic	🔒	3 wk ago	Nicolae Tarla	-
Escalate	···	Escalate	Topic	🔒	3 wk ago	Nicolae Tarla	-
Goodbye	···	Goodbye	Topic	🔒	3 wk ago	Nicolae Tarla	-
Greeting	···	Greeting	Topic	🔒	3 wk ago	Nicolae Tarla	-
Lesson 1 - A simple topic	···	Lesson 1 - A simple topic	Topic	🔒	3 wk ago	Nicolae Tarla	-
Lesson 2 - A simple topic with a condition and variable	···	Lesson 2 - A simple topic with a condition and variable	Topic	🔒	3 wk ago	Nicolae Tarla	-
Lesson 3 - A topic with a condition, variables and a pre-built e	···	Lesson 3 - A topic with a condition, variables and a pre	Topic	🔒	3 wk ago	Nicolae Tarla	-
Lesson 4 - A topic with a condition, variables and custom entit	···	Lesson 4 - A topic with a condition, variables and cust	Topic	🔒	3 wk ago	Nicolae Tarla	-
Start over	···	Start over	Topic	🔒	3 wk ago	Nicolae Tarla	-
Thank you	···	Thank you	Topic	🔒	3 wk ago	Nicolae Tarla	-
Usage Type	···	Usage Type	Bot entity	🔒	3 wk ago	Nicolae Tarla	-
Use system and sample topics	···	Use system and sample topics	Topic	🔒	3 wk ago	Nicolae Tarla	-

Figure 12.9 – Solution including a chatbot

Now you are ready to export your solution from the current development environment and deploy it to other environments.

As a rule, if you are deploying to another development environment, you want to export the solution as unmanaged. For any deployments to test in production, you want to deploy as a managed solution.

In order to increase efficiency and provide better value to our customers, let's have a look next at capabilities around monitoring existing Power Virtual Agents.

Monitoring the success of Power Virtual Agents

Microsoft has put together a pretty robust **Analytics** package for Power Virtual Agents. You can get to it from the chatbot editor, by selecting the **Analytics** menu option on the left side of the screen, as shown in the following screenshot:

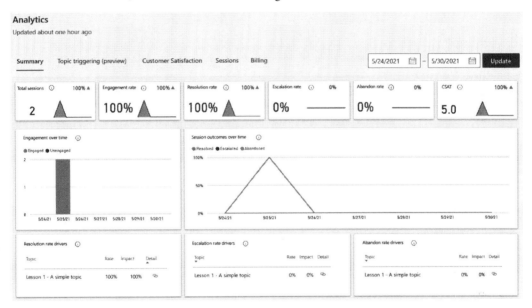

Figure 12.10 – Power Virtual Agents chatbot Analytics

You can take advantage of these reports to determine things such as the following:

- Engagement over time
- Session outcomes over time
- Resolution rates
- Escalation rates
- Abandon rates

Based on these observations, you can determine items and places to make improvements to your chatbot. This should result in improvements to your chatbot. Monitoring pre and post changes will give you a good indication of whether the updates are in fact beneficial to the overall performance of your chatbot.

In addition to monitoring for performance and making improvements to your chatbot, another aspect is to monitor for customer satisfaction. This is an important aspect as it will provide you with direct ratings from the actual customers using your chatbot. Your standard customer satisfaction dashboard is presented in the following screenshot:

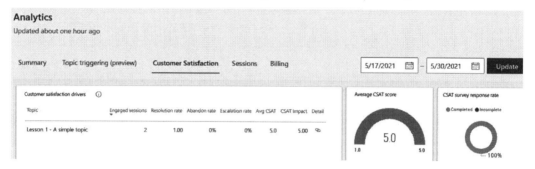

Figure 12.11 – Customer Satisfaction dashboard

Here you can track the overall satisfaction, the scoring over time, as well as the ratings by individual topics.

While creating Power Virtual Agents, it is not uncommon for some unexpected scenarios to creep up. Let's see next how to troubleshoot some common issues.

Troubleshooting issues

At the time of writing, Microsoft has issued a notice about the following known issues:

- **Permission issues**: The error message **You do not have permissions to any environments. Please get access from an administrator.** will be presented when you cannot create a chatbot in the current environment. You should create an environment where you have access to create new chatbots.

- **Environment is missing from the list of environments**: This will happen if your environment does not have a database created. Power Virtual Agents requires a database in the chatbot environment. You must go to the admin console, select the environment, and choose the option to create a database in the environment. Each environment can only have no database or one database. If your environment is in a region that does not support this functionality, you should create a new environment in a region that supports these features.

Microsoft will continue to update the listing of known issues as more are resolved or new ones are introduced. It is always a good idea to keep an eye on the official documentation.

This documentation is released through both `https://docs.microsoft.com` and the release notes for both annual release cycles for the platform.

Summary

In this final chapter, we reviewed the administration aspects of Power Virtual Agents. We looked at basic chatbot management, managing active chatbots, making modifications to existing chatbots, as well as monitoring their performance and troubleshooting issues.

With the knowledge gained from this book, you should now be ready to start creating successful chatbots for your organization. You will soon become the resident expert on this topic within your organization.

Packt.com

Subscribe to our online digital library for full access to over 7,000 books and videos, as well as industry leading tools to help you plan your personal development and advance your career. For more information, please visit our website.

Why subscribe?

- Spend less time learning and more time coding with practical eBooks and Videos from over 4,000 industry professionals

- Improve your learning with Skill Plans built especially for you

- Get a free eBook or video every month

- Fully searchable for easy access to vital information

- Copy and paste, print, and bookmark content

Did you know that Packt offers eBook versions of every book published, with PDF and ePub files available? You can upgrade to the eBook version at packt.com and as a print book customer, you are entitled to a discount on the eBook copy. Get in touch with us at customercare@packtpub.com for more details.

At www.packt.com, you can also read a collection of free technical articles, sign up for a range of free newsletters, and receive exclusive discounts and offers on Packt books and eBooks.

Other Books You May Enjoy

If you enjoyed this book, you may be interested in these other books by Packt:

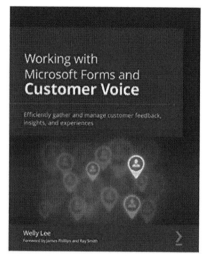

Working with Microsoft Forms and Customer Voice

Welly Lee

ISBN: 978-1-80107-017-1

- Get up and running with Microsoft Forms and Dynamics 365 Customer Voice services
- Explore common feedback scenarios and survey best practices
- Understand how to administer Microsoft Forms and Dynamics 365 Customer Voice
- Use Microsoft Forms or Dynamics 365 Customer Voice to monitor your survey results
- Set up the Microsoft Forms app for Teams for conducting live polls
- Automate feedback collection and follow-up actions

Microsoft 365 and SharePoint Online Cookbook

Gaurav Mahajan, Sudeep Ghatak

ISBN: 978-1-83864-667-7

- Get to grips with a wide range of apps and cloud services in Microsoft 365
- Discover ways to use SharePoint Online to create and manage content
- Store and share documents using SharePoint Online
- Improve your search experience with Microsoft Search
- Leverage the Power Platform to build business solutions with Power Automate, Power Apps, Power BI, and Power Virtual
- Enhance native capabilities in SharePoint and Teams using the SPFx framework
- Use Microsoft Teams to meet, chat, and collaborate with colleagues or external users

Packt is searching for authors like you

If you're interested in becoming an author for Packt, please visit authors.packtpub.com and apply today. We have worked with thousands of developers and tech professionals, just like you, to help them share their insight with the global tech community. You can make a general application, apply for a specific hot topic that we are recruiting an author for, or submit your own idea.

Hi!

I am Nicolae Tarla, author of *Empowering Organizations with Power Virtual Agents*. I really hope you enjoyed reading this book and found it useful for increasing your productivity and efficiency in Power Virtual Agents.

It would really help me (and other potential readers!) if you could leave a review on Amazon sharing your thoughts on *Empowering Organizations with Power Virtual Agents*.

Go to the link below or scan the QR code to leave your review:

```
https://packt.link/r/1801074747
```

Your review will help me to understand what's worked well in this book, and what could be improved upon for future editions, so it really is appreciated.

Best Wishes,

Nico Tarla

Index

99479528R00136